Gender and Distance Education

This book investigates the intersection of gender and distance education from a feminist perspective and explores their contemporary innovative interfaces in Indian and international contexts.

The key issues raised here include a re-investigation of the democratizing potential of distance education from a gendered perspective (especially in developing countries such as India), feminist pedagogical perspectives on the notion of transactional distance, the relationship between masculinity and gerontology from the perspective of non-traditional modes, and the inter-relationships between gender and social media from a distance education perspective. As opposed to the conventional, physical classroom, the virtual classroom often occupies a de-privileged space in feminist pedagogical discussions, since it appears to align itself less easily with feminist praxes which encourage a free, intellectual exchange between teachers and students. By opening up various facets of the relationship between gender, distance education and feminist pedagogy, the book foregrounds the critical need to re-visit preconceived, unfavourable assumptions about this relationship and proposes mutually productive inter-linkages. It does so in the context of contemporary circumstances defined by the increasing use of virtual technology, the ongoing need for democratization of higher education and the constraints posed by consumerist trends.

Lucid and topical, this Focus volume will be useful to scholars and researchers of higher education, open and distance education, feminist pedagogy, gender studies, feminism, masculinity, and women's studies as well as practitioners and policymakers working in the education sector.

Anu Aneja is Professor in the School of Gender and Development Studies at Indira Gandhi National Open University, New Delhi, India. She earned a Bachelor's degree in French from Jawaharlal Nehru University and a doctorate in Comparative Literature from Pennsylvania State University. She taught for several years at Ohio Wesleyan University in the United States, where she was the recipient of the Rebecca Brown Professor of Literature award. She was also awarded the Beatrice B. Maines fellowship for research in women's studies at the University of California, Berkeley. She has published in the areas of contemporary French, francophone and Indian literatures, feminine discourses, feminist perspectives on mothering, and feminist theory and pedagogy. Her most recent co-authored publication (with Shubhangi Vaidya) is *Embodying Motherhood: Perspectives from Contemporary India* (2016). She is currently editing a collection [illegible] women's and gender studies in India.

Gender and Distance Education

Indian and International Contexts

Edited by Anu Aneja

LONDON AND NEW YORK

First published 2019 by Routledge

2 Park Square, Milton Park, Abingdon, Oxfordshire OX14 4RN
52 Vanderbilt Avenue, New York, NY 10017

Routledge is an imprint of the Taylor & Francis Group, an informa business

First issued in paperback 2019

British Library Cataloguing-in-Publication Data
A catalogue record for this book is available from the British Library

Library of Congress Cataloging-in-Publication Data
A catalog record for this book has been requested

ISBN: 978-1-138-61542-7 (hbk)
ISBN: 978-0-367-47944-2 (pbk)

Typeset in Sabon
by Apex CoVantage, LLC

Contents

List of illustrations vi
Notes on contributors vii
Acknowledgements viii

Introduction 1
ANU ANEJA

1 **Combining feminist pedagogy and transactional distance to create gender-sensitive technology-enhanced learning** 10
CLEM HERMAN AND GILL KIRKUP

2 **Blending in: reconciling feminist pedagogy and distance education across cultures** 30
ANU ANEJA

3 **Online education as 'vanguard' higher education: exploring masculinities, ideologies, and gerontology** 55
LAUREN ILA MISIASZEK

4 **Feminist pedagogy and social media: a study on their integration and effectiveness in training budding women entrepreneurs** 80
MANGALA VADIVU VIVAKARAN AND NEELAMALAR MARAIMALAI

Index 108

Illustrations

Figures

2.1 MAWGS: programme structure at a glance 41
4.1 The research design used for the present study 88
4.2 Screenshots of the virtual workshop conducted for the study 90
4.3 The pie chart representing the content analysis of the online discussions 92
4.4 Knowledge assessment of the participants before and after attending the workshop 93
4.5 The pie charts representing the agreement level of the participants regarding various factors influencing women entrepreneurship in India 94
4.6 Satisfaction level of the participants 95
4.7 Participants' confidence boost after attending the workshop 96
4.8 Participants' preference over online and conventional workshop 96
4.9 Engagement level of all the posts generated in the workshop 97
4.10 Engagement level of session-wise posts generated in the workshop 98
4.11 Network structure visualisation of the two-day virtual workshop 99

Tables

2.1 MAWGS disaggregated data, 2014–2016 43
2.2 MAWGS need assessment for online forum, 2015 survey 48
4.1 Schematic representation of the experimental study 88
4.2 Session schedule of the workshop 89

Contributors

Clem Herman is Director of eSTEeM, the Centre for STEM Pedagogy at the Open University, UK. Her research focuses on gender and careers in STEM.

Gill Kirkup worked at the Open University, UK, until her retirement in 2015. She researched and published in the areas of gender and distance education, and gender and technology.

Neelamalar Maraimalai is Assistant Professor in the Department of Media Sciences, Anna University, India. She has authored five books on media including *Media Law and Ethics* (2010) and *Radio Programme Production* (2017).

Lauren Ila Misiaszek is Associate Professor at the Institute of International and Comparative Education, Faculty of Education, Beijing Normal University, China.

Mangala Vadivu Vivakaran is a PhD research scholar at the Department of Media Sciences, Anna University, India. Her areas of interest include social media, education and learning technologies.

Acknowledgements

I am deeply indebted to the contributors for responding in such rich ways to a subject I thought worth addressing—the complex relationship between gender and distance education, especially from the vantage point of feminist pedagogy. I am also grateful to all of them—Clem Herman, Gill Kirkup, Lauren Ila Misiaszek, Mangala Vadivu Vivakaran and Neelamalar Maraimala—for the generous patience and perseverance they have shown during the editing and review process.

Much of what I have learnt about gender and distance education is owed to my teaching experience at Indira Gandhi National Open University (IGNOU). The institution has offered a space for a blending of feminist pedagogy and distance education that has been critical for reflecting upon this relationship. I am grateful to my colleagues at IGNOU for previous opportunities to present some of my ideas in preliminary form, and to the library staff for their ready assistance with 'remote access' to research materials.

For her professionalism and positive feedback, I am very thankful to Shoma Choudhury, Commissioning Manager, Routledge, Taylor & Francis Group, New Delhi.

Finally, I am grateful to Taylor & Francis Ltd for their permission to re-publish the four articles presented here. The articles were previously published in two consecutive issues of *Gender and Education* (volume 29.6 and volume 29.7, 2017) for which I was the guest editor and are reprinted here by permission of the publisher, www.tandfonline.com.

Clem Herman and Gill Kirkup, 'Combining feminist pedagogy and transactional distance to create gender sensitive technology enhanced learning', *Gender and Education*, 29, no. 6: 781–789, October 2017, http://dx.doi.org/10.1080/09540253.2016.1187263

Anu Aneja, 'Blending in: reconciling feminist pedagogy and distance education across cultures', *Gender and Education*, 29, no. 7: 850–868, December 2017, https://doi.org/10.1080/09540253.2016.1237621.

Lauren Ila Misiaszek, 'Online education as "vanguard" higher education: exploring masculinities, ideologies, and gerontology', *Gender and Education*, 29, no. 6: 691–708, October 2017, http://dx.doi.org/10.1080/09540253.2016.1225015.

Mangala Vadivu Vivakaran and Neelamalar Maraimalai, 'Feminist pedagogy and social media: a study on their integration and effectiveness in training budding women entrepreneurs', *Gender and Education*, 29, no. 7: 869–889, December 2017, https://doi.org/10.1080/09540253.2016.1225008.

Introduction

Anu Aneja

Distance education, especially in its most recent online and digital avatars, has opened up a world of educational opportunities internationally by bringing higher education within the reach of previously disenfranchised and marginalized learners, including many women and non-traditional students. Despite such an inclusive mandate and attentiveness to gender concerns, the relationship between distance education and feminist pedagogy has not been an easy one. Viewed through a feminist lens, the notion of 'distance' inherent in open and distance education continues to defy certain accepted feminist principles fostered in the tangible and interactive physical space of the classroom. In recent years, the increasing use of technology for educational purposes has led to shifts in the nature of debates around the virtues of competing pedagogies, which now include open, distance, virtual and blended modes, alongside face-to-face teaching. These debates have altered feminist perceptions of distance education, even as the shape of the traditional classroom continues to morph with new advances in technology and communication, in turn influencing gender dynamics in teaching and learning environments. Under these circumstances, it becomes increasingly urgent to examine distance education practices from a gendered perspective, and to find ways of resolving its somewhat ambivalent relationship with feminist pedagogy. Equally imperative is the growing need to address the gendered dimensions of open and distance education. These include its potential for democratization of education through equal access and inclusion, its outreach to women and non-traditional learners and entrepreneurs, and its intersections with changing notions of gendered identity, including masculinity. This said, cross-cultural differences as well as infrastructural inequities, especially those between developed and developing nations and urban and rural settings, must be taken into account in any analysis of how distance education and gender come to be interpolated in specific contexts.

This small collection of articles was originally conceived with the aim of highlighting a few of these pressing issues. Intended to elaborate on the fluid interface between gender, distance education and feminist pedagogy across the world, the four articles presented here share this underlying thematic unity and were previously published in two consecutive volumes of *Gender and Education* (2017, 29(6) and 29(7)). The collection juxtaposes Indian and international contexts as a way of exemplifying these questions in widely different cultural contexts; at the same time, it is not in any way intended to be exhaustive of the range of issues such a subject may generate. In bringing together these few examples in a common-focus volume, it is hoped that the questions they foreground will inspire other efforts to push forward the existing scholarship on gender and distance education.

By way of introducing the context for these themed articles, I offer a very brief overview of the place of gender within distance education in what follows, especially from the perspective of changing feminist evaluations. Feminist responses to distance and virtual pedagogies have undergone a sea change since the time distance education universities were primarily viewed and projected as digital factories. Quite obviously, these were perceived as largely antithetical to feminist mandates which attempted to make the personal political through experiential and interactive learning within the classroom. Moreover, feminist teachers who struggled to re-shape the masculinised structure of the university classroom by various means of democratization (such as student-centric interactions, a focus on personal, experiential knowledge, encouraging debate, and actively creating spaces that included women's voices) may have been naturally appalled at the remoteness of the distance learner from her teacher. Additionally, the consumerist models of knowledge dissemination associated with private, open universities (especially in the west) were completely at odds with feminist modes of knowledge construction and transaction, and especially so with progressive notions of transgressive education such as expounded upon by bell hooks (1994). Although not entirely unfounded, this perception of distance education tended to conceive of 'distance' as inherently masculist and consequently, distance education institutions as non-democratic consumerist spaces driven by market forces, unconcerned with the ideological commitments to diversity and inclusion that lie at the heart of feminist ethics. Further, the older 'correspondence course' model of distance education prevalent in many parts of the world until the mid-twentieth century had seemingly closed off avenues for the lively exchange of viewpoints that is supposed to occur in the exemplary feminist classroom, severing the two almost completely.

Since the 1960s, a few significant developments have taken place that have brought about a shift in the antithetical locations of feminist pedagogy and distance education and made room for a re-conceptualization of the interpolation of gender with distance education. On the one hand, pedagogical practices within distance education have evolved from an earlier dependence on print material, postal deliveries and multi-media to an increasing reliance on virtual modes of teaching and learning, setting into motion entirely novel connotations of the term 'distance'. On the other hand, a critical self-appraisal of feminist pedagogy has led to the realization that gender, race, class and caste hierarchies may continue to persist in seemingly democratic spaces such as the feminist classroom, and in fact, may even be exaggerated in such locations. These developments have led to a re-thinking of prevalent biases against distance education and its close ties with technology, and a re-evaluation of feminist pedagogies that are now more open to experimenting with technology and virtual spaces. As observed by Natasha Patterson (2009) in her appraisal of distance education, even though the women's studies classroom is perceived as a relatively safe space, it remains embedded within the larger masculinist structure of higher education institutions. In contrast, the remote, virtual space of online interactions that might signal a cold, detached environment, may in fact facilitate unfettered exchanges that help to overcome gender, race, class and caste barriers. Whether or not online spaces discourage or promote hierarchical interactions and present safe spaces for women and other marginalized learners has generated persuasive opinions and fascinating research on both sides of this debate (see, for instance, Von Prummer 2004; Kirkup 1996; Murray et al. 2013; Kendall 1998; Richards 2011; Schweitzer 2001). Further, ongoing feminist interrogations of the cultural construction of gendered identities have led to revised understandings of femininity as well as masculinity. Nuanced understandings of gender continue to shape contemporary research in the area of gender and distance education, from the perspective of learners as well as teachers.

More recently, a closer scrutiny of the notion of 'transactional distance' (as elaborated upon by Michael Moore in 1997) has led to the growing recognition that all teaching–learning environments must confront 'distance' in one form or another and more significantly, that distance, in itself, may not be an entirely bad thing. In increasingly digital environments, the idea that physical distance leads to a separation and lack of communication between teachers and learners is losing its dominance, as more and more of us learn to communicate virtually with the help of technology, and to experience lives in which the virtual and real repeatedly spill into each other. Once we acknowledge that 'distance' is inherent in any interactive environment, whether physical or virtual, the term begins to lose its previous negative associations. This has led feminist scholars to revise previously held reservations against virtual and distance learning pedagogies and to carve out a space for the exploration of the interplay between gender and distance education. Democratization, inclusiveness, knowledge construction and co-creation in student-centred classrooms, which have been the hallmarks of feminist ethics, are now also recognized as inherent aspects of the founding principles of distance education. The fact that open and distance education was primarily conceived as a social experiment for inclusive outreach (especially so in highly populated developing countries) may have been overlooked in the early perfunctory dismissals it faced. Especially in societies where the social fabric is riven by sharp economic and other structural inequities, the original mandate of distance education universities offered the hope of reducing inequalities and improving employment possibilities through mass-based opportunities for higher education. In India, for instance, this was envisioned through a promotion of inclusive outreach across barriers of gender, class, caste, region, disability and rural–urban divides, that is, education for all. Seen from this perspective, the potential to bring about a rapprochement between feminist goals and distance education practices becomes all the more evident.

This said, it must also be recognized that any proposed alliance between feminist ethics and distance education continues to be constrained by various factors emerging from cultural, regional and institutional variations, as well as pedagogical praxes that are in place. In many cases, an adherence to older behaviourist models of distance learning with a high degree of reliance on print material makes it challenging to move beyond delivery-based methods that tend towards a freezing of knowledge in pre-determined information capsules; such models reduce the space for an interrogation of gender and other structural biases that can be debated in interactive environments. As already noted, it is equally critical to remain alert to the dangers of a re-inscription of gender, race, class and caste hierarchies that may be operative in online spaces. When print and multi-media modes are replaced or supplemented by online modes, different degrees of regional-, gendered-, race- and class-based digital divides may continue to determine their success at any given place and time. The fluctuating relationship between technology and the gender gap in different regional contexts will be an important determinant of the outcome of online modes of education in terms of inclusivity. In India, for instance, persisting urban–rural, gender, class, religion and caste inequities could cast a shadow upon the tall claims of open universities regarding the level of inclusiveness achieved through digital interactions. Evidently, the specific socio-cultural circumstances that delimit the operational accomplishments of virtual and online teaching praxes in different countries and regions of the world need to be taken into account in any consideration of gender dynamics within localized situations. It may be useful, in the context of locating the relationship between gender and technology in regional environments, to keep in mind the notion of 'placed resources' as introduced by Mastin Prinsloo (2005) who argues for a contextual adaptation of virtual pedagogy to maximize its benefits through experimentation and adaptation. Particularly in countries like India, limited infrastructural resources and a deep-rooted gender gap in the fields of higher education, employment and entrepreneurship are factors to take into account in any investigation of gender and distance education. Other factors that need to be considered include institutional pressures exerted by increasingly consumerist trends of higher education in capitalist economies. It remains largely true that numerous private institutions offering distance and online courses in different parts of the world continue to operate what may still be termed 'digital diploma mills', an accusation first made by David Noble (1998) and repeated by feminist scholars like Chandra Mohanty (2003). Emergent capitalist environments in developing countries such as India, and the resultant privatization and commodification of higher education present ongoing challenges to distance education's original democratization mandate. When seen through a feminist lens, these challenges continue to act as roadblocks in any potential reconciliation between feminist ethics and distance learning pedagogical environments.

Notwithstanding such limitations, the advantages promised by the mandate of distance education with respect to gender inclusivity should act as a catalyst for an exploration of alternative models that can inspire innovative experimentations at the intersections of feminist pedagogy and distance education. Although open and distance learning institutions may not always be successfully implementing non-elitist values, the inclusive foundations of distance education philosophy and its commitment to undoing gender and other structural inequities certainly provide a strong basis for building bridges that could be used strategically for strengthening such a partnership. Consequently, we are witness now to concerted efforts by feminists who seek to overcome such hurdles through a refusal of consumerist knowledge transaction from within the institutional boundary, and who experiment with the more adaptable facets of distance education pedagogy to harmonize these with feminist praxis. For instance, distance education's valorization of student-centric, interactive learning processes and of knowledge co-creation would be some of the aspects that appear particularly amenable from the standpoint of feminist pedagogy.

The four articles presented in this volume exemplify a few such explorations in Indian and international contexts. As may become evident even from this limited selection, feminist pedagogy has come to engage with distance education in exploratory and affirmative ways in very different parts of the world. At the same time, marked cultural, economic and infrastructural differences and the specific character of localized relationships between gender and distance education result in strikingly different contours of these explorations. The two articles stemming from the Indian context bring to the fore some of the specific challenges as well as possibilities enabled by a rapprochement between feminist pedagogy and distance education, while taking into account specific socio-cultural determinants and structural inequities of gender, class and caste. In doing so, they serve as a reminder that neither distance education nor feminist ideologies operate in a vacuum, and that feminist pedagogical experimentations must take into account regional factors such as the varying degrees of gender gaps and gendered digital divides in different localized circumstances. Viewed within their specific environments, these different approaches open up new ways of transacting education within the democratic frameworks upheld by distance education, and of advancing future scholarship in this area. As well, they can bring about revised understandings of the interface between gender identities and online pedagogy, from the perspectives of both students and teachers.

As noted above, a critical notion in any such enterprise is that of 'transactional distance', suggestive of an inherent psychological distance between teacher and student in any pedagogical environment. In the first article of this collection, 'Combining feminist pedagogy and transactional distance to create gender-sensitive technology-enhanced learning', Clem Herman and Gill Kirkup argue against certain assumptions, present within both feminist pedagogy and transactional distance, which have tended to focus on the negative aspects of distance. By positing geographical distance in a positive light the authors interrogate the idea that distance is necessarily disadvantageous, especially to women students. Further, by highlighting women's success with distance education, they show how the notion of distance, when used to one's advantage (for instance, when it helps to create 'space for reflection'), can in fact serve to undo unequal gender/power relations in the conventional classroom environment. Using the Open University's STEM courses (UK), they assess the impact of such courses on women learners to contend that distance education continues to provide enhanced educational opportunities, especially for poorer women, through innovative uses of technology.

The notion of transactional distance is also taken up in my article, 'Blending in: reconciling feminist pedagogy and distance education across cultures.' Beginning within an international context, I attempt to unravel how feminist pedagogy's suspicions of distance education have been largely overcome on the basis of a shared democratic ethic as well as the insertion of the pervasive notion of 'transactional distance' which cuts across all forms of teaching and learning. Revised understandings of 'distance' and 'virtual' further help to stem the gap between the two. In the varied circumstances created by globalization in developing countries, such reconciliations may evolve in hybrid forms. I explore some ramifications of this in the context of India, where infrastructural constraints and consumerist trends necessitate contextualized pedagogical strategies. Using the example of a master's degree programme at the Indira Gandhi National Open University, I show how one such innovative 'blended' approach was adopted to overcome specific institutional challenges in the interest of advancing feminist pedagogical principles within a distance education setting. Caste, class and gendered inequities which characterize the Indian social fabric present challenges to any effort at making higher education more inclusive. The fact that a higher percentage of urban learners are able to access distance education programmes in gender studies must give us pause for thought regarding learners in rural areas who remain marginalized due to a prevalent digital divide, lack of awareness or other factors. These factors, of course, continue to be examined by distance education scholars. Yet, it is also encouraging to see that the percentage of rural learners is steadily increasing in such courses, as evidenced in the particular example dealt with in this article. Overall, the widening reach of distance education gender studies programmes across urban–rural and gender barriers, augurs well for future partnerships between feminist pedagogy and distance education.

It is equally important to examine gendered dimensions of distance education pedagogy from the perspective of educators, just as it is vital to include perspectives on masculinity when we speak of 'gender'. In her article, 'Online education as "vanguard" higher education: exploring masculinities, ideologies, and gerontology', Lauren Ila Misiaszek draws our attention to the significant relationship between pedagogues, masculinity and gerontology within distance education environments. Misiaszek argues that non-traditional higher education online settings present critical sites to examine how pedagogues navigate such spaces. She employs 'sketches' (incomplete, potential starting points) as a way of exploring the 'future directions' of three specific sub-fields: masculinities and higher education, masculinities online, and masculinities and aging, using critical feminist perspectives. A strategic case study of an older male educator employed in two for-profit universities (online and brick and mortar) is used as the methodological basis for a consideration of some of these complex convergences, which Misiaszek analyses with the help of a Freirean lens. Based on the four sketches that outline this particular educator's pedagogical experiences, the article attempts to open up a critical engagement with complex social identifiers in distance education. This potential signals rich possibilities for an ongoing engagement between feminist pedagogies and distance education, posited here as a 'vanguard' space. In many ways, this vanguard space emblematizes the newly emerging spaces of experimentation opened up by the exploration of distance education from a gendered lens, and is an apt metaphor for drawing together the various viewpoints presented in this collection.

While the first three articles are located within the realm of higher education, the fourth highlights the role of virtually supported educational opportunities for women entrepreneurs. In 'Feminist pedagogy and social media: a study on their integration and effectiveness in training budding women entrepreneurs', Mangala Vadivu Vivakaran and Neelamalar Maraimalai show how a culturally entrenched gender gap, and deep-rooted gender roles and responsibilities, obstruct women from availing equal educational opportunities and exploring entrepreneurial careers. The authors examine the possibility of overcoming such impediments by combining online learning and feminist pedagogy, both of which offer learner-centric, participatory and collaborative environments. They show how an integration of Web 2.0 and feminist pedagogy can create a virtual feminist environment for budding entrepreneurs. Using data collected from an online workshop conducted on the basis of feminist pedagogical principles, they analyse the effectiveness of social media platforms as a pedagogical tool for women entrepreneurs. The authors' contention that virtual learning environments supported by feminist principles can help in reducing the gender gap in educational and entrepreneurial domains is an important roadmap for the future, especially in developing countries.

The digital revolution within educational settings has brought us to the cusp of a new era where technology and online education, on both sides of the so-called digital divide, will increasingly interrogate and challenge the idea of geographical distance as a separation between students and teachers. As previously noted, this has particular bearing on questions of gender and pedagogy. From a feminist pedagogical perspective, it is a critical juncture—to carry forward this awareness and explore the future interface between gender and distance education, while remaining alert to the caveats that emerge in varied regional and cultural contexts. This volume is intended as a small step in this direction.

References

hooks, b. 1994. *Teaching to Transgress: Education as the Practice of Freedom.* London: Routledge.

Kendall, Lori. 1998. Meaning and Identity in 'Cyberspace': The Performance of Gender, Class, and Race Online. *Symbolic Interaction* 21, no. 2: 129–153.

Kirkup, Gill. 1996. The Importance of Gender. In *Supporting the Learner in Open and Distance Learning*, eds. R. Mills & A. Tait, 146–165. London: Pitman.

Mohanty, Chandra T. 2003. Privatized Citizenship, Corporate Academies, and Feminist Projects. In *Feminism Without Borders*, 169–189. London: Duke University Press.

Moore, Michael Grahame. 1997. Theory of Transactional Distance. In *Theoretical Principles of Distance Education*, ed. D. Keegan, 22–38. New York: Routledge.

Moore, Michael Grahame. 2007. The Theory of Transactional Distance. In *Handbook of Distance Education*, 2nd edition, ed. M. Moore, 89–105. New Jersey: Lawrence Erlbaum Associates.

Murray, Jessica, Deirdre Byrne & Leandra Koenig-Visagie. 2013. Teaching Gender Studies via Open and Distance Learning in South Africa. *Distance Education* 34, no. 3: 339–352.

Noble, David F. 1998. Digital Diploma Mills: The Automation of Higher Education. *Monthly Review* 49, no. 9. Accessed 16 April, 2018. https://monthlyreview.org/1998/02/01/digital-diploma-mills/.

Patterson, Natasha. 2009. Distance Education: A Perspective from Women's Studies. *Thirdspace: A Journal of Feminist Theory & Culture* 9, no. 1.

Prinsloo, Mastin. 2005. The New Literacies as Placed Resources. *Perspectives in Education* 23, no. 4: 87–98.

Richards, Rebecca S. 2011. 'I Could Have Told You *That* Wouldn't Work': Cyberfeminist Pedagogy in Action. *Feminist Teacher* 22, no. 1: 5–22.

Schweitzer, Ivy. 2001. Women's Studies Online: Cyberfeminsm or Cyberhype? *Women's Studies Quarterly* 29, no. 3/4: 187–217.

Von Prummer, Christine. 2004. Gender Issues and Learning Online. In *Learner Support in Open, Distance and Online Learning Environments*, eds. Jane E. Brindley, Christine Walti & Olaf Zawacki-Richter, 179–192. Oldenburg: University of Oldenburg, Center for Distance Education.

1 Combining feminist pedagogy and transactional distance to create gender-sensitive technology-enhanced learning

Clem Herman and Gill Kirkup

Introduction

Historically, distance education programmes have been very attractive to women; and women students have been very successful in their distance education studies. Yet theories of feminist pedagogy and of transactional distance in education would suggest that women students would be alienated by distance education methods and struggle to succeed. In this paper we explore how distance can, for women students, provide an opportunity to engage with learning, and if we understand the affordance provided by distance, we can use it creatively to develop a new feminist pedagogy that brings gender sensitivity to technology-enhanced learning.

Historians usually trace the origins of large-scale distance education to the nineteenth century (Holmberg 1995) when the combination of widespread literacy, low-cost printing, and reliable postal systems provided the ideal environment for the development of 'correspondence education'. Women who were either excluded formally from educational institutions or informally by their responsibilities in the home were some of the earliest distance learning students. Anna Ticknor is credited with being the first person to try and personalise distance education in her Boston-based Society to Encourage Study at Home. She encouraged teachers and students to write to each other, as well as engaging with the monthly guided readings and tests that formed[1] the curriculum. When the Open University (OU) was established in the UK and began to deliver courses in the early 1970s, women very quickly became a majority of the student body, as well as having better course completion rates than male students (Woodley and McIntosh 1980). The large-scale enrolment of women in distance education in the UK and elsewhere was unexpected, but can be explained by women's prior lack of opportunity to engage in other kinds of education

(Lunneborg 1994); however, women's successful completion rates need more explanation. At a time when, all over the world, distance education institutions were being established, and hundreds of thousands of women were registering for and completing programmes of study taught by distance methods, a theory and practice of feminist pedagogy was developing that behaved as if all teaching involved a face-to-face classroom experience. Late twentieth-century feminist pedagogic theory argued that education was inherently gendered as a cultural institution and that radical pedagogy needed to explicitly develop critical consciousness in students (Freire 1973) through group discussion (Thompson 1983). Critical consciousness was often described as 'consciousness raising' in 1980s feminism, and usually seen as a crucial aspect of feminist pedagogy. At first glance, it would seem to be impossible to create the opportunity for the kind of consciousness-raising activities promoted in the feminist education literature in distance education because of the structural difficulties of enabling the kind of interpersonal interactions that were common to many early feminist classrooms (Culley and Portuges 1985). The success of women students in early paper-based distance education models brings into question this emphasis on interpersonal interaction, as being a key condition for feminist pedagogy.

The challenges for interpersonal interaction identified in feminist theory were also identified in the field of distance educational theory as 'transactional distance' (Moore 1997). Transactional distance theory argues that it is not spatial or temporal distance (in distance learning) between learners and teachers per se that matters, but it is the interruptions that these cause in communication (i.e. the two-way 'transactions' between the learners, the teacher, and the content) in which misunderstandings can develop and grow. Both transactional distance theory and feminist pedagogy have at their core an implicit assumption that the ideal learning environment is one where teachers and students are co-located in time and space, and that it is this co-location that offers the best opportunity for clear and open communication amongst everyone engaged in the learning process. While feminist pedagogy addresses the nature of gendered power in this classroom context, transactional distance theory does not. One kind of 'distance' produced in face-to-face transactions is that of gender/power. This has been described by social theorists such as Hofstede (1998) as the social distance created culturally by gender, and by feminists as the male power which culturally silences women and limits women's autonomy. This power has been exercised through all other cultural institutions including educational institutions.

In this paper we draw on empirical evidence from the OU, to challenge both feminist pedagogy and transaction distance theory to explain why distance learning initiatives have been so successful for women. We suggest that geographic or spatial distance can be a positive factor that can serve to decrease other aspects of transactional distance that can occur in one-to-one or group communication, in particular those that create alienation and the silencing of women produced by the operation of unequal gender/power relations, between teachers and students and amongst students. For women historically (and in some countries still in the present day), the operation of gender/power has excluded them from education and even when women get access to education, gender power can negatively impact on their performance. Feminist pedagogy has promoted women-only spaces as the learning design solution to the negative impact of gender/power; however, we argue that distance education can produce, and has produced, other kinds of learning designs that use the positive aspects of 'distance' to allow women to overcome the negative aspects of gender/power in a mixed-sex learning environment. The danger in both transactional distance theory and feminist pedagogy, of focusing on increasing the social and communication activities of education through the use of other media, could in fact increase the negative effect of gender/power on women if the positive aspects of spatial and temporal distance are not understood.

Transactional distance

When 'first-generation'[2] distance learning programmes were set up, the term 'distance' was used in its common sense geographical/spatial meaning – that is, that students and teachers were located a long way from each other. This distance was initially bridged by 'correspondence': the printed content materials that were sent to students, and later communication that also included broadcast radio and television programmes. It was also bridged in the way that students, their teachers/tutors, and assessors corresponded with each other via, for example, exchanges of documents: letters, course work, assessment feedback, and later by telephone and by face-to-face tutorials. By the 1970s, Moore (1973) was theorising the nature of this distance as beyond the simple spatial. He identified the various separations (such as that between teacher and student), produced by geographic distance, and labelled these examples of 'transactional distance'. Transactional distance, he argued, is 'a psychological and communications space to be crossed, a space of potential misunderstanding' (Moore 1997, 22).

He identified three aspects of education in which transactional distance has a detrimental impact on student engagement: it can interfere with positive dialogue which is influenced by the medium as well as the design of a communication and the behaviour of those communicating; it can limit learning design or programme structure which involves communication and dialogue; and finally, it limits learner autonomy, which is about the extent to which any learner is able to take responsibility for his/her own learning.

The literature on transactional distance has never suggested that there could ever be circumstances in which this distance is beneficial to the learner; the presumption has been implicit that separation has only negative consequences. Yet, for many groups of learners who have been disempowered in traditional educational systems (including some social and racial groups, and people with disabilities, as well as women), distance education has had very positive consequences. Distance education literature has focused on exploring the negative impact of transactional distance, by comparing measures such as student completion rates for courses taught by distance learning with face-to-face methods. The lower completion rates for distance learning are identified by Simpson as part of the cause for what he (2013) has called the 'distance education deficit'. However, both Moore and Simpson argue that this deficit can be overcome by appropriate interventions in student support systems, and by the better use of new media. What this critical position on distance has not been able to explain is the very high ratings that the OU has received from students completing the UK National Student Survey.[3] The University has received overall student 'satisfaction' ratings that match those of the most prestigious face-to-face universities in the UK, as well as scoring the highest for student satisfaction with assessment and feedback from tutors. There has also been less work done comparing the performance of different kinds of students within a distance education context, and the most recent work has focused on the use of large data sets to predict individual student success rather than an analysis of particular factors contributing to it (Prinsloo, Slade, and Galpin 2012).

Since the advent of Internet-based distance education, the stress has been on bridging transactional distance through technological and design solutions. The newest work on learning analytics follows this trajectory. It has been argued that we need instead to look at different 'generations' of learning theory i.e. cognitive-behaviourist, social constructivist, and connectivist pedagogy (Dron and Anderson 2012) to avoid seeing both the problem and the solution as technical. Researchers have also not accounted for the successful student who uses the 'separation' inherent in distance learning in a positive way, to create space for reflection, to disengage from non-productive power relations in the learning context, and to self-manage their time and energy. These positive attributes of transactional distance have, we argue, been beneficial for women in our institution, and in many places in the world, such 'separation' has allowed women to engage with education without having to engage with the highly gender discriminatory nature of male-dominated learning environments.

Feminist pedagogy

Feminist pedagogy has its roots in the liberation theories of adult learning (Freire 1970, 1973) and in the small group methods used for the sharing and analysis of experience – labelled consciousness raising – some of which was politically oriented and some of which came from the humanistic psychology, and reciprocal peer-counselling movements of the 1960s (Rogers 1961). Added to this were feminist critiques of mainstream psychology (Belenky, Goldberger, and Tarule 1986; Gilligan 1982). From the viewpoint of 2015 feminist pedagogic practices can look very like constructivist learning, but only if the political and ideological underpinnings of feminist pedagogy are forgotten – especially its rationale for action: to challenge gender power.

There is a consistent ideological framework to feminist pedagogy (Webb, Allen, and Walker 2002). Morley (2002) has an excellent summary of this. The central core of feminist pedagogy, she argues, is a challenge to the authoritarianism of 'masculine' modes of pedagogy. It has an emphasis on the creation of knowledge through dialogue and includes reflexivity by the learner. Pedagogy is a social as well as cognitive activity and there are always connections made between pedagogical dis/empowerment and sociopolitical power: that is, knowledge is power. Feminist pedagogy is driven by emancipatory intentions. Personal/experiential knowledge is often valued as highly as abstract/propositional knowledge. There is an emphasis on the links between personal and social change. Inter-connections between ideology, power, and culture are made visible and challenged within and outside the classroom. A feminist teacher accepts that educational practices, as well as knowledge, are socially constructed, and action, including that of teaching, should be informed by critical engagement with theory (praxis). The traditional feminist classroom emphasises participation and negotiation (hooks 1994, 2003). Students are invited to see themselves as shapers of knowledge and learning. Feminist academic practice crosses the boundaries of disciplines. There is an emphasis on the links between personal and social change. Feminist pedagogy looks only at individual student autonomy primarily within the perspective of the overall gender power relations of society. However, as Henderson (2013) notes, feminist pedagogy is an evolving approach and not a fixed set of attributes.

> Rather than reduce feminist pedagogy to a single, fixed list of characteristics, with a canon of authoritative references to follow up . . . feminist pedagogy [is] fragmented, . . . Originating from and belonging to different people and places . . . a continually developing phenomenon that invites teachers and students to contribute to its evolution.
>
> (Henderson 2013)

Distance education as a form of feminist pedagogy has not always been visible to those theorists and practitioners who focused almost exclusively on face-to-face classrooms. This concentration on face-to-face engagement, and synchronous communication focuses attention on interpersonal interactions (see Crabtree, Sapp, and Licona 2009). This has been picked up by feminist educators who have experimented with using innovative learning technologies such as virtual worlds to provide an enhanced sense of presence that enables supportive group interactions. Feminist pedagogy, we argue, needs to embrace the potential of distance education to reach and teach women (and men) in different ways, and – like transactional distance theory – it needs to move beyond a notion that distance has always been disadvantageous. Creating more opportunities to interact using new media could simply result in strengthening unequal gender/power relations that had been positively weakened by the reduction in synchronous interpersonal communication in earlier forms of distance learning.

There has been a danger that feminist pedagogy has become restricted to being a discourse of resistance to the system, rather than a source of tools and strategies for producing liberatory education for women who take advantage of the system. The focus on face-to-face learning and teaching and on the interpersonal interactions of students and teachers has implied that other kinds of non-classroom educational experiences were less valuable. This has meant that learning mediated through other media: print, broadcasting, and more recently information and communication technologies, has been seen as of minor interest or importance, even non-feminist. However, the creation of transactional distance through distance learning methods can effectively bypass some of the gender power relations that often exist in traditional classroom settings; distance learning can be a form of feminist pedagogy. Moore and others writing about transactional distance have presumed that classrooms are places of positive dialogue, while feminist educators know that this has not been the case for women. Interactions between teachers and students have had a negative impact on learning. Feminist pedagogy acknowledges this, but creates strategies for changing the environment inside the classroom. It rarely takes the more radical position of arguing for an alternative to the classroom. Yet this might be where feminist educators could make the more radical impact. It was interesting, for example, to see in the early days of the OU the relatively large numbers of women studying traditionally male subjects like engineering, because they could do so 'privately' without having to overtly challenge the traditional gendering of subject areas through their embodiment in a traditional classroom, and as we show by the examples we discuss later in the paper, science, technology, engineering, and maths (STEM) subjects have been where distance education has been particularly successful for women.

At this point, we acknowledge that educational policy advocating women's distance education has sometimes been based on anti-feminist assumptions about women's primary domestic responsibilities and women's inability to engage in the public sphere of education. This kind of argument was often drawn from a pragmatic assessment made by governments or even NGOs. Such a rationale for distance education can reinforce and polarise existing gender roles, and therefore run counter to the aims of feminist pedagogy (Bergviken, Rensfeldt and Riomar 2010). But we are not arguing for initiatives for women to exist ONLY in distance education – they should be part of a whole movement towards changing societies where women are disadvantaged or trapped by rigid gender norms. It would also seem cruel to argue that special educational initiatives for women should NOT be offered in societies where gender inequality is embedded in other areas. The hostility to single-sex distance education also seems to ignore the emancipatory potential of education per se, where the content studied drives social change, rather than the way study is organised. Arguments about the political appropriateness of distance education for women parallel that about single-sex education to which we return in a subsequent section.

Positive action

Feminist staff at the OU recognised from the early years of the institution that women were coming to the University for education to change their lives (Kirkup 1988). As an institution dedicated to 'openness', the

University has been willing to design programmes for different student populations where the need was understood. In this paper, we focus largely on what has been achieved for women wanting to move into or return to traditionally masculine areas of study and employment.

Positive action as a strategy to support the inclusion of women in areas of learning and work in which they are traditionally under-represented has close connection with feminist pedagogical approaches and aspirations, and was one of the earliest areas to receive funding for special programmes for women. For example, training programmes and centres to train women in IT and other traditionally male-dominated skills were set up in the UK and elsewhere in the EU during the 1980s and 1990s (Page and Scott 2001; Rommes, Faulkner, and van Slooten 2005; Vehviläinen and Brunila 2007). Acquiring non-traditional skills in manual trades and new technologies was empowering not only in terms of the practical skills they offered, but also because they served to disrupt gendered expectations (Herman 2001). Having challenged one aspect of their identities and expectations, women often found themselves able to contemplate changes in other parts their lives. This has been a continued theme reported in the experiences of women studying through distance education (Kirkup and Whitelegg 2012; Lunneborg 1994; von Prummer 2005).

Models of feminist distance education

As we have just argued in the previous section, one way to provide for women in any educational space is through single-sex education. This has been one of the characteristics of positive action initiatives. The Sex Discrimination Act 1975 in the UK allowed for positive action in education and training to address labour market gender inequalities. This meant that organisations could advertise women-only or men-only training courses for work where it could be shown that few or no people of that sex have done that kind of work in the previous year.[4] This allowed for the development of single-sex courses in STEM areas of the OU curriculum, although not in other areas where you might expect it: such as Gender Studies.

Particularly in technology and manual skills training, such an environment provides a transformative space for women to do gender differently away from normative gendered constraints in relation to technological practice (Ellen and Herman 2005). Malcolm, Jackson, and Thomas (2011) argue that women-only spaces perform an important role in identity formation for women lifelong learners at key transformational periods – 'learning through participation in women-centred spaces enables resistance through subversive strategies including resistance to ascribed identities and re-construction of new ones' (Malcolm, Jackson, and Thomas 2011, 249). For women who are not employed (e.g. those taking a career break), accessing learning in a women-only space enables the development of self-esteem that is often lost during periods outside of paid work, especially when their primary role as mothers has undermined their professional confidence (Ellen and Herman 2005; Herman 2014; Herman et al. 2011).

In technical and scientific fields, single-sex education or training is claimed as an emancipatory strategy that frees women and girls from the competitive and critical gaze of men and boys, providing a stepping stone to entering a mixed-sex environment on a more equal footing. This applies not only to girls, but also to older learners and returners. However, in STEM fields there is a danger that such approaches can also reinforce gender stereotypes by labelling women as 'deficient' in technological or scientific skill and emphasising their lack of confidence, therefore falling into the trap that some single-sex distance education provision has fallen into seeming to support the notion that women are not able to engage equally with men in an educational context. Single-sex education and training thus remain contentious, criticised by some as perpetuating gender binaries and inequalities.

More closely targeted initiatives aimed at specific groups of women with shared characteristics and needs (such as women returners, for example) seem to produce the best outcomes as they are 'deepening the transformative potential for their target groups' (Sørensen, Faulkner, and Rommes 2011).

Feminist pedagogical initiatives at the OU

We now turn to consider in detail some of the initiatives developed at the OU to support women, and explore how different models of distance education have been used to achieve feminist pedagogical aims, and at the same time used the positive aspects of transactional distance. Some of these have been focused on areas where women are under-represented in employment such as STEM areas or management roles, while others have been within the gender and women's studies curriculum area.

The earliest scheme offered by the OU for women only was the Women in Technology (WIT) scheme. Initially, WIT was a scheme to retrain and update women who were graduates in STEM, but who had been out of the workforce because of family responsibilities. It was so successful that after the first three years it was expanded to include women who wanted to enter STEM work but who had no previous qualifications (Kirkup and Swarbrick 1986). Women on the scheme were funded to register on OU courses in STEM areas and were allocated additional tutorial support as well as attending a weekend school. The activities of the weekend school oriented the women to OU study, and also used well-established face-to-face feminist pedagogic classroom-based methods to encourage the women to reflect on their own career trajectories, and the role of gender in shaping their lives and careers, and in the fields of employment they intended to re-enter. In the 1980s, OU distance learning technologies included paper-based materials, television and radio broadcasting, audio materials (on tape), and some computer-based activities using networked teletype machines located in local study centres, supported by local tutors. After the single-sex weekend school, all the women on the scheme studied their STEM courses in mixed-sex 'tutor groups', receiving exactly the same learning materials as the men. There was concern that this might produce a sense of isolation for students:

> This isolation of pre-internet distance education was a well-recognised problem, and a great deal of effort was spent encouraging students to find ways to keep in contact with each other after the residential experience.
>
> (Herman et al. 2011)

However, women in the OU were more successful than men in passing their courses, which suggested that, at least in comparative terms with men, this isolation was not a detriment to their study. Women on the WIT scheme were able to study traditionally male subject areas alongside male students without having to be 'embodied' in an overwhelmingly male classroom. This transactional distance from fellow male students, and from the male presence of a teacher, allowed, we argue, the women to have a closer and more satisfying engagement with the content of study. WIT ended after six years, benefitting over 600 women, most of whom returned to employment within a few years of being on the scheme (Kirkup and Swarbrick 1986).

In 2002, the UK government commissioned a report about the numbers of women dropping out of and not returning to STEM careers (People, Science and Policy 2002). As a result, the OU was funded to develop an online course (Return to SET) which between 2005 and 2011 was taken by over 1000 women who were seeking to return to work after a career break. This was the first large-scale online course of its kind, and presented the opportunity to adapt previous approaches from face-to-face women's development programmes within an online environment. The course was employment focussed and involved students in assessing their professional and personal needs, and developing their own strategies to return to work. As part of this, they were introduced to ideas about the gendering of work in STEM occupations (Herman et al. 2011). The first section of the course consisted of an extended reflection of prior experiences and career achievements, including an analysis of life events that had shaped their careers. This also involved online asynchronous discussions on themes such as work–life balance, and in that sense could be seen to be part of the tradition of consciousness raising that had been the mainstay of feminist pedagogical approaches of the 1970s and 1980s, bringing personal experiences into the virtual classroom that enabled a deeper understanding of the gendered constraints that had shaped their own careers. For many of the women, this sharing of experience and 'being in the same boat' were powerful and transformative processes, even perhaps emancipatory in their impact. This was a model which tried to implement into an asynchronous online environment many of the techniques and activities used in the feminist face-to-face classroom, and with some success, although it is the case that many more women choose not to 'speak' in an online environment than choose to do so in a face-to-face context. The existence of non-speaking 'lurkers' is one that has always been seen as a problem by those designing and running online learning. However, research has shown that many students have very good reasons for 'lurking' and do so while actively engaging in learning (Preece, Nonnecke, and Andrews 2004).

Another method or strategy that has been widely adopted to support women into STEM is that of role models. The presence of positive role models who have succeeded in progressing to senior levels in STEM professions increases women's sense of entitlement to combine a career with family care responsibilities (Herman and Lewis 2012). The 'Return to SET' course materials included stories of nine women returners, and illustrated their experiences using audio clips and photos, covering practical as well as psychological/emotional issues that they had encountered. 'Visiting experts' from industry were invited to question and answer sessions in an asynchronous online forum. This all demonstrates that role models can be successfully presented at a distance through texts, audio, and video and that engaging synchronously and face-to-face with them is not a necessary requirement. The 'Return to SET' courses were short (only 10 weeks long) and followed a tradition of similar short professional development programmes.

The first women-only short course at the OU had been a course called 'Women into Management'. This was designed for junior women who were aiming to progress their careers and move into managerial roles. The OU has, through the education it provides in the Business School, enabled many people working in junior administrative positions to progress to more senior management positions. In the 1980s it recruited many fewer women students in this area. In 1987 women were 43% of all OU students on undergraduate courses, but they comprised only 15% of those on finance courses and 33% on personnel courses. Research had indicated that there were many women working in administrative and clerical positions who wanted job promotion but did not have the confidence to embark on a business studies course. They needed a bridge. Women into Management was designed to be that bridge and specifically to provide a bridge to the first-level management studies course (Kirkup and Smith 1987). The curriculum was very similar in content to that of the later women returners' courses, although it predated Internet-delivered learning and was text and video based. As with the 'Return to SET' course, it drew on what had been learned from women's development programmes elsewhere and focussed on the personal development needs for women who wanted to move into, or progress in a career. It also included many development activities which aimed to increase students' confidence as well as help them make a realistic assessment of their skills and development needs. Students also studied a section on the way gender operates in the workplace, to sensitise them to organisation and cultural issues and give them a context to understand their own employment history. This course ran for nine years between 1986 and 1994, over which time 3065 women studied it.

The discussion of the above courses shows the extent that one national distance teaching university provided emancipatory courses for women, leading to career opportunities as well as personal development, and which included feminist content, and variants of feminist pedagogy while taking advantage of the positive aspects of distance.

As well as these courses designed specifically to support women's career development, the OU also ran Women/Gender Studies (WGS) courses. These were not designed to be single-sex courses, and were also open to men (although 94% of the 8000 students who studied the courses between 1982 and 1999 were women). These courses could be studied as part of the bachelor's degree or taken outside that formal structure, as a one-off course for interest or for professional development. Each course was designed by a team of OU feminist scholars and external experts brought in as consultants to contribute their expertise to specific sections of the courses. These two courses are described in Kirkup and Whitelegg (2012) which examines the challenges produced by these courses and their legacy and in Kirkup,

Whitelegg, and Rowbotham (2015) which examines the capabilities students developed whilst studying, contextualised within the British educational and employment landscape available to these students as they were growing up.

These courses provided something that was only possible for distance education; the content created for the course was available outside the classroom, to anyone who wanted to access it. The teaching materials were published as high-quality study guides by the University and were also available to purchase by the general public. The specially produced and collected readings for the courses were co-published as text books by commercial publishers and so were widely available in bookshops nationwide and beyond. This publishing activity gave visibility to the large number of feminist scholars who had worked together on each course over a three-year period to prepare the materials for the students to study. These were feminist courses, about feminism, and it was expected that the content rather than the learning design would be what transformed the women studying them. It could be argued that this activity was not the co-production of knowledge advocated by theorists of feminist pedagogy, since it did not include contributions by students, but these specially designed texts were a co-production by the teachers of the course, which produced a new contribution to feminist scholarship.

The possibility of open-access web publishing now makes it possible for all educational institutions with the resources to open all their materials to the public. The most recent educational initiative for women at the OU is a new Open Educational Resource (OER) entitled Reboot Your STEM Career. This has no assessment, neither does it have a fixed start or end date. As an OER it is open to both men and women and thus operates on a different model to the previous courses. It is too early to say how this will be received or what the take up will be. As with many new models of online education including massive open online courses, this OER poses difficult questions about the purpose, impact, or efficacy of such efforts. The challenge for feminist educators is to learn from the successes of prior distance learning models and examine how these technological developments and changes in educational models can be embraced and utilised to further women's education, and at the same time expand the notion of what constitutes feminist pedagogy.

Impact on women students

We have presented a set of initiatives designed to embody feminist pedagogy in a distance learning context, and discussed the operation of transactional distance in these initiatives; but the proof that these initiatives have been good for women is the outcomes they have. Two recent follow-up studies with OU women students who had participated in some of the initiatives described above looked in more detail at the impact of the courses in terms of their feminist pedagogical characteristics and aims and to what extent they were able to successfully bridge the transactional distance between the learners and teachers (or indeed whether that made any difference). In each of the cases discussed above, the curriculum was created by a group of feminist practitioners/educators, but not by the students themselves. While the student voice was enabled when the course had a face-to-face component or an online interactive discussion function, the content was fixed prior to the enrolment of students. However, it would be wrong to presume from this that this content was then absorbed unchanged or undigested by each student. The activities designed for the students and the assessments they did included a great deal of reflection and reflexive autobiographical work (Herman and Kirkup 2008). This is where each student co-creates the knowledge that she takes away; this is where a student is 'changed' by learning. It is simplistic to locate this only in classroom debates.

If we look at focus in feminist pedagogy on the use of experience as a resource, the reflective activities of the Return to SET courses could be construed as fitting within this category. But in WIT, for example, where the women were taking part in mainstream STEM modules, there was little in the way of space for them to use their previous experience. Indeed, we would argue that this can be a particular gendered problem in STEM education as a large body of research has shown that STEM teaching assumes a set of prior experience gained while growing up as a boy with boyish hobbies and experiences – (playing with construction toys such as Meccano or fixing a car engine and more recently, playing computer games) and this creates a barrier for women students who do not have similar backgrounds (Margolis and Fisher 2002). Thus, disciplinary differences can affect the efficacy of feminist pedagogical approaches. So rather than experience, feminist interventions to attract girls to science or technology education have assumed the opposite, that there is limited informal prior experience to build on, but instead transferable interests and aspirations may be more appropriate (such as stressing the social value and impact of STEM careers). Thus, a basic presumption of feminist pedagogy is challenged in STEM education.

There is no question that for many of the women who attended the courses described above, what they experienced was transformative learning, whether this was explicitly from the content of the curriculum or from the learning experience itself. From the recent evaluation of the WGS courses, it was clear that many women experienced a sense of empowerment and renewed confidence, which they still remarked upon nearly 30 years later (Kirkup, Whitelegg, and Rowbotham 2015).

Similarly, students on the Return to SET courses were often affected in life-changing ways, even though the curriculum did not present as having overtly feminist content. The course was advertised and described as a route back into work. As this student observed, they were not coming to learn about gender or feminism.

> I'm sure it was completely unintended, but the focus of the course, and the choice of examples and language, have turned me into a feminist.
>
> (Student evaluation – anonymous)

To some extent, any women-only courses where the creators are feminists with feminist aims have such a hidden curriculum. The quote also suggests that the student understood the intention of the course creators and facilitators, namely to raise consciousness of gendered disadvantage in employment opportunities. Thus as feminist educators, we have been visible to the student, she has recognised our intentions even though we had not made these overt, her consciousness was raised, and she understood her gendered position in STEM.

The positive distance of distance education – the newest feminist pedagogy

The experience of the OU distance education courses for women challenges many of those attributes that are usually associated with feminist pedagogy. In examining and analysing how our educational initiatives have engaged with the generally accepted characteristics of feminist pedagogy as outlined, we have identified that our projects do not neatly map onto these categories and this raises questions about how far these established understandings of feminist pedagogies and characteristics, as outlined for example by Henderson (2013), are appropriate to the newest system of learning or to all disciplines. Moreover, we would contend that feminist pedagogy as generally understood has a particular historical location and new theoretical models need to be developed to take account of modern technology-enhanced learning environments as well as new practices of learning design. Distance learning is no longer the poor relation of face-to-face education, it is being adopted as central to new designs for learning such as the 'flipped classroom' (Educause 2012). Distance education has led the field of learning design. Distance is indeed now a positive feature of learning for many institutions.

Feminist criteria for the co-creation of content were developed originally to be used within a particular type of learning environment and embody a rather simplistic notion of content and knowledge. If we see co-creation happening between each individual and content as well as within group interactions with content, then we free ourselves from the notion that real-time interventions by groups of students in classroom equivalent spaces are necessary for learning to be valid.

Our evidence from follow-up studies with our students suggests that distance education interventions offered in the OU since the 1980s have been very successful and have had empowering and sustained impact for many of the participants. We would contend that this is the most important facet of feminist pedagogy, rather than any particular 'recipe' of characteristics as earlier writers have suggested.

One of the reasons for the success we have evidenced is, we believe, that distance learning offers potential advantages over face-to-face classroom encounters and allows for the personalisation of learning, and for defusing gender/power distance. Women in distance learning contexts are removed from the male gaze, by not being obliged to inhabit embodied spaces where they are objectified as 'the other' rather than simply being a member of the student group. In situations such as mixed-sex STEM classes, women's inclusion as a minority gender is less obvious. Distance allows not only for spaces where misunderstandings develop (Moore 1973, 1997), but also for spaces where disrupting and reflection can take place. This opens up new possibilities of escaping from the domination of male authorities in texts, and in the social behaviours of fellow students and teachers. Distance needs to be welcomed as a new tool in feminist pedagogy.

Transactional distance is ultimately not the miles covered by letters in the mail, the strength and speed of an Internet network connection, or the time taken to respond to an asynchronous email message, it is a reflection of how engaged the student is with learning. Transactional distance can exist in a classroom, where for example the students sitting within feet of each other come from cultural backgrounds and bring sets of experiences so different from the teacher, and from each other that communication often breaks down. We have argued that gendered power differences produce greater transactional distance for female than male students, particularly in male-dominated disciplines such as STEM. The solution to the problems of transactional distance is not always to create the opportunity for more interaction between people, if that interaction brings unequal power with it. The stress on the importance of group learning in some distance learning models can imply that students perhaps have a greater obligation for the learning of fellow students than they have for themselves and their own comfort, and it can ignore the gendered or other power dynamics, even within an online learning environment. Many of our women students have enjoyed and benefitted from NOT being in the virtual classroom with male students on the same course, but equally in some cases enjoyed NOT being with other female students. This is the hard message that both theories of feminist pedagogy and theories of transactional distance have to come to grips with as we move into a new age of widespread and ubiquitous technology-enhanced learning.

Notes

1 See more about Anna Ticknor on the website of the Ticknor Society: http://www.ticknor.org/Anna.shtml (accessed 16.06.2015).
2 Garrison (1985) was the first person to differentiate 'generations' in distance education systems, the first being that of correspondence-only education. The second generation is characterised by the use of mass broadcast media. The third generation incorporates online, interactive, that is, two way and more, communication systems.
3 See national survey analysis from 2005 onwards: http://www.hefce.ac.uk/lt/nss/results/.
4 The Sex Discrimination Act allows training organisations to take positive action measures to advertise women-only or men-only training courses for work where it can be shown that few or no people of that gender have done that kind of work in the previous year – http://www.equalityhumanrights.com/.

References

Belenky, M. F., N. R. Goldberger, and J. M. Tarule, eds. 1986. *Women's Ways of Knowing: The Development of Self, Voice, and Mind*. New York: Basic Books.
Bergviken Rensfeldt, A., and S. Riomar. 2010. "Gendered Distance Education Spaces 'Keeping Women in Place'?" In *Gender Issues in Learning and Working with Information Technology: Social Constructs and Cultural Contexts*, edited by S. Booth, S. Goodman, & G. Kirkup, 192–208. New York: Hershey.
Crabtree, R., D. A. Sapp, and A. Licona. 2009. *Feminist Pedagogy.Looking Back to Move forwards*. Baltimore: John Hopkins University Press.
Culley, M., and C. Portuges, eds. 1985. *Gendered Subjects. The Dynamics of Feminist Teaching*. London: Rouledge and Kegan Paul.
Dron, J., and T. Anderson. 2012. "The Distant Crowd: Transactional Distance and New Social Media Literacies." *International Journal of Learning and Media* 4 (3–4): 65–72. doi:10.1162/IJLM_a_00104.

Educause. 2012. "7 Things You should Know about . . . Flipped Classrooms." https://net.educause.edu/ir/library/pdf/ELI7081.pdf.

Ellen, D., and C. Herman. 2005. "Women's Training Revisited: Developing New Learning Pathways for Women IT Technicians Using a Holistic Approach." In *The Gender Politics of ICT*, edited by J. Archibald, J. Emms, F. Grundy, J. Payne, & E. Turner, 251–264. London: Middlesex University Press.

Freire, P. 1970. *Pedagogy of the Oppressed*. New York: Seabury Press.

Freire, P. 1973. *Education for Critical Consciousness*. New York: Herter and Herter.

Garrison, D. R. 1985. "Three Generations of Technological Innovations in Distance Education." *Distance Education* 6 (2): 235–241. doi:10.1080/0158791850060208.

Gilligan, C. 1982. *In a Different Voice: Psychological Theory and Women's Development*. London: Harvard University Press.

Henderson, E. F. 2013. "Feminist Pedagogy." Gender and Education Website, January. Accessed July, 2015. http://www.genderandeducation.com/resources/pedagogies/feminist-pedagogy/.

Herman, C. 2001. "From Visions to Reality: Changing Women's Perspectives at the Village Hall." *ACM SIGCAS Computers and Society* 31 (4): 15–22.

Herman, C. 2014. "Returning to STEM: Gendered Factors Affecting Employability for Mature Women Students." *Journal of Education and Work*. doi: 10.1080/13639080.2014.887198.

Herman, C., B. Hodgson, G. Kirkup, and E. Whitelegg. 2011. "Innovatory Educational Models for Women Returners in Science, Engineering and Technology Professions." In *Gendered Choices: Learning Work Identities in Lifelong Learning*, edited by I. Malcolm, 53–68. Dordrecht: Springer Academic Press.

Herman, C., and G. Kirkup. 2008. "Learners in Transition: The Use of e-Portfolios for Women Returners to Science, Engineering and Technology." *Innovations in Education and Teaching International* 45 (1): 67–76.

Herman, C., and S. Lewis. 2012. "Entitled to a Sustainable Career? Motherhood in Science, Engineering, and Technology." *Journal of Social Issues* 68 (4): 767–789.

Hofstede, G., ed. 1998. *Masculinity and Femininity: The Taboo Dimension of National Cultures*. Thousand Oaks, CA: Sage.

Holmberg, B. 1995. "The Evolution of the Character and Practice of Distance Education." *Open Learning: The Journal of Open, Distance and e-Learning* 10 (2): 47–53. doi:10.1080/0268051950100207.

hooks, b. 1994. *Teaching to Transgress: Education as the Practice of Freedom*. London: Routledge.

hooks, b. 2003. *Teaching Community: A Pedagogy of Hope*. London: Routledge.

Kirkup, G. 1988. "Sowing the Seeds: Initiatives for Improving the Representation of Women." In *Towards New Horizons for Women in Distance Education*, edited by K. Faith, 287–312. London: Routledge.

Kirkup, G., and R. Smith. 1987. "Women into Management." A Report on the Development, Piloting and Evaluation of a Distance Taught Course for Aspring Women Managers, Produced by the Open University School of Management and funded by the Manpower Services Commission (pp. 68). Milton Keynes: Open University.

Kirkup, G., and A. Swarbrick. 1986. "Women in Technology." A Report to the Training Division of the Manpower Services Commission on the First Year of Option 1 for Women with No Technological Qualifications Who Wish to Enter Technology (pp. 65). Milton Keynes, UK: Open Univ. Inst. of Educational Technology.

Kirkup, G., and E. Whitelegg. 2012. "The Legacy and Impact of Open University Women's/Gender Studies: 30 Years on." *Gender and Education* 25 (1): 6–22. doi:10.1080/09540253.2012.728569.

Kirkup, G., L. Whitelegg, and I. Rowbotham. 2015. "The Role of Women's/Gender Studies in the Changing Lives of British Women." *Gender and Education* 27 (4): 430–444. doi:10.1080/09540253.2015.1015500.

Lunneborg, P. W. 1994. *OU Women: Undoing Educational Obstacles*. London: Cassell.

Malcolm, I., S. Jackson, and K. Thomas. 2011. "Policy Challenges: New Spaces for Women's Lifelong Learning." In *Gendered Choices: Learning, Work, Identities in Lifelong Learning*, edited by S. Jackson, I. Malcolm, & K. Thomas, 245–252. London: Springer.

Margolis, J., and A. Fisher. 2002. *Unlocking the Clubhouse: Women in Computing*. Cambridge: MIT Press.

Moore, M. G. 1973. "Toward a Theory of Independent Learning and Teaching." *The Journal of Higher Education* 44 (9): 661–679. doi:10.2307/1980599.

Moore, M. G. 1997. "Theory of Transactional Distance." In *Theoretical Principles of Distance Education*, edited by D. Keegan, 22–38. London: Routledge.

Morley, L. 2002. "Lifelong Yearning. Feminist Pedagogy in the Learning Society." In *Gender, Teaching and Research in Higher Education*, edited by G. Howie, & A. Tauchert, 86–98. London: Ashgate Press.

Page, M., and A. Scott. 2001. "Change Agency and Women's Learning New Practices in Community Informatics." *Information, Communication & Society* 4 (4): 528–559. doi:10.1080/13691180110097003.

People Science and Policy Ltd. 2002. *Maximising Returns to Science, Engineering and Technology Careers*. London: Department of Trade and Industry.

Preece, J., B. Nonnecke, and D. Andrews. 2004. "The Top Five Reasons for Lurking: Improving Community Experiences for Everyone." *Computers in Human Behavior* 20 (2): 201–223. doi:10.1016/j.chb.2003.10.015.

Prinsloo, P., S. Slade, and F. Galpin. 2012. "Learning Analytics: Challenges, Paradoxes and Opportunities for Mega Open Distance Learning Institutions." Paper presented at the Proceedings of the 2nd International Conference on Learning Analytics and Knowledge, Vancouver, British Columbia, Canada.

von Prummer, C. 2005. *Women and Distance Education: Challenges and Opportunities*. Abingdon: Taylor & Francis.

Rogers, C. R. 1961. *On Becoming a Person*. Boston, MA: Houghton Mifflin.

Rommes, E., W. Faulkner, and I. van Slooten. 2005. "Changing Lives: The Case for Women-Only Vocational Technology Training Revisited." *Journal of Vocational Education & Training* 57: 293–317.

Simpson, O. 2013. "Student Retention in Distance Education: Are We Failing our Students?" *Open Learning: The Journal of Open, Distance and e-Learning* 28 (2): 105–119. doi:10.1080/02680513.2013.847363.

Sørensen, K. H., W. Faulkner, and E. Rommes, eds. 2011. *Technologies of Inclusion. Gender in the Information Society*. Trondheim: Tapir Academic Press.

Thompson, J. L. 1983. *Learning Liberation. Women's Response to Men's Education*. London: Croom Helm.

Vehviläinen, M., and K. Brunila. 2007. "Cartography of Gender Equality Projects in ICT: Liberal Equality from the Perspective of Situated Equality." *Information, Communication & Society* 10 (3): 384–403. doi:10.1080/13691180701410067.

Webb, L., M. Allen, and K. L. Walker. 2002. "Feminist Pedagogy: Identifying Basic Principles." *Academic Exchange Quarterly* 6: 67–72.

Woodley, A., and N. E. McIntosh. 1980. *The Door Stood Open*. Abingdon: Taylor & Francis.

2 Blending in

Reconciling feminist pedagogy and distance education across cultures

Anu Aneja

Introduction

Distance education (DE) evolved in the middle of the twentieth century in response to the need to overcome the inherent shortcomings of correspondence education, which had relied almost entirely on the ability of learners to complete coursework through self-study. Correspondence learners had limited or no contact with teachers and peers and faced isolation and lack of support in completing their course of study. In order to reduce students' sense of remoteness, distance learning introduced a highly stratified structure of geographically spread out regional centres and study centres, where students could interact directly with counsellors and administrators in local settings. These centres served as intermediary contact points between faculty and students to bring the learning experience nearer to a 'classroom-like' situation. By opening up higher education avenues for working adults and other non-traditional learners, DE quickly became an effective way of providing educational access to multitudes of learners who may have otherwise remained deprived of such opportunities.

One of the most significant achievements of DE has been its democratic outreach to women and other marginalised groups, and it has consequently invited feminist attention and investigation. While acknowledging DE's inclusive and learner-centric functioning, feminist educators have equally interrogated its limitations from the perspective of feminist pedagogy which tends to privilege face-to-face (f2f) contact and has been suspicious of the notion of 'distance'. Despite such reservations, possibilities of an alignment with DE have been variously explored, especially with the recent shift towards technology driven education. In the west, attempts have been made to reconcile feminist pedagogy with DE by disrupting real/virtual binaries. Contesting previously held views which equated mass-based DE institutions with 'digital diploma mills',[1] many feminist educators have persuasively argued the case for the proximity between feminist and DE pedagogies, and upset the 'sage on the virtual stage' metaphor by promoting the notion of the online, participatory learner.

The first part of the article investigates these issues within a broad, international framework to outline feminist pedagogy's conflicted relationship with Open & Distance Learning (ODL), as well as to examine strategies which have effectively closed the gap between the two, especially through a denial of rigid boundaries between the real and the virtual.

In the second part, I explore this relationship in developing countries, more specifically, India. Here, although a common democratising mandate continues to shore up the association between feminist pedagogy and DE, consumerist leanings of ODL institutional structures imply that feminist pedagogy will present substantive challenges to the former's normative impulses. In India, DE is primarily seen as an affirmative social experiment in providing mass-based educational outreach to marginalised groups. However, institutional compulsions for profitable, high enrolment programmes pose particular challenges and remain at odds with the democratisation mandate. Further, infrastructural and other constraints imply that efforts at a rapprochement must be differently mapped, calling for suitable innovations in the interest of feminist pedagogical aims.

Women's Studies courses, which pursue democratisation both at a systemic and a substantive level, offer a good testing ground for such efforts. I illustrate this through an MA programme in which an innovative course design was combined with a blended pedagogical approach. Rather than offering this as a universally applicable model, my intent is to instantiate one possible pedagogical strategy for enabling a productive engagement between ODL and feminist pedagogy in the hope of provoking other attempts for doing so.

Going the distance between feminist and ODL pedagogies

In this section, I attempt to delineate the complex relationship between ODL and feminist pedagogy in order to sketch a broad international canvas against which a similar alliance could then be mapped out in the specific context of India. Feminist pedagogy's efforts to ally with ODL are reflective of strong, shared values at the core of this alliance – most prominently, a common democratising mandate. Consequently, recent years have been witness to feminist pedagogy's attempts to address its concerns about ODL as a viable pedagogical approach. In the west, these attempts have been enabled to a large extent by the dislodging of previously secure binaries of online/offline, and an exploration of hybrid spaces resulting in a softening of feminist pedagogy's earlier qualms about the remoteness of distance learning modes. In the subsequent section, I will investigate the contours of a similar alliance in the context of developing countries.

A brief overview of feminist pedagogy's attempts to draw closer to DE can help trace its changing stance towards the latter. From an early scepticism, feminist pedagogy has gradually come to embrace many aspects of virtual and online learning which are conducive to feminist ethics. The former denigration of distance learning on the basis of unfavourable comparisons with f2f instruction led to a privileging of the physical space of the classroom seen as a prerequisite to, and enabler of, the kind of experiential learning crucial to feminist pedagogy. Consequently, the split between the two modes remains an unresolved binary that informs teaching practices associated with Women's Studies. Conventional feminist wisdom which questions the viability of DE (often confused with correspondence courses) arises from some obvious reservations about the latter's potential to establish personal contact, and its lack of space for validation of individual, subjective experiences which may emerge in synchronous, participatory classroom discussions.

From this dichotomous perspective, f2f instruction has over time become the yardstick against which DE must measure up. Efforts made by ODL educators to engage students through participatory strategies have consequently been viewed as a 'replication' of classroom dynamics (Patterson 2009), with some arguing for a postmodern undoing of binaries (Larreamendy-Joerns and Leinhardt 2006, 579–580). In a bid to overcome the disparagement that DE is subjected to within ivory tower conceptions of higher education, it has been proposed that rather than trying to prove that DE is 'as good as' f2f teaching we need to go beyond and prove that it is *better* than the latter (Larreamendy-Joerns and Leinhardt 2006, 594).

However, from a feminist viewpoint, the race for pedagogical ascendancy and 'oneupmanship' may only impede the integration of favourable aspects of both modes. Rather, such a competitive perspective may be gainfully set aside through innovative locally contextualised pedagogical permutations which foreground learning, irrespective of the mode. I will dwell on this issue further in the specific context of India.

What then, we may begin by asking, keeps feminist pedagogy at a 'distance' from DE? Historically, some key hurdles have prevented a rapprochement between the two. A fundamental sticking point has been the notion of an insurmountable chasm between teachers and students, implied in distance learning. Some of the ways in which ODL has been variously defined and understood, very often at the expense of the distinction between 'open' and 'distance' learning, throw light on this issue. One such definition, provided by UK Open University, proposes that 'although the terms are often used interchangeably', 'open learning is an umbrella term for any scheme of education or training that seeks systematically to remove barriers to learning' while distance learning 'is one particular form of open learning in which tutors and learners are separated by geographical distance'.[2]

Singularly distinguished on the basis of *geographical space*, distance learning thus constitutes a sub-set of open learning, while the umbrella term under which it is subsumed leaves the door 'open' for all possible modes of instruction. The dichotomy between open and conventional education is further problematised by the notion of 'transactional distance' which, according to Moore (1997), denotes physical, manifest qualities as well as notional aspects of 'distance' – 'a psychological and communications space to be crossed, a space of potential misunderstanding between the inputs of instructor and those of the learner'. Moore points out that 'in any educational program, even in face-to-face education, there is some transactional distance' (22).

Transactional distance undercuts the binaries between f2f/DE, real/virtual to reveal 'distance' as an overarching, invisible presence within all teaching spaces. Its dual axes, constituted by the teacher and the student, are measured by the degree of dialogue between them: 'as dialog increases, transactional distance decreases' (Moore 2007, 94). By doing away with the hierarchical pecking order of f2f vs. DE, transactional distance opens the latter to the possibility of constructivist adaptations since 'dialogue' becomes a common feature of all instructional modes. This is a far cry from the perceptions of a proximity to behaviourist theory[3] upon which DE and online pedagogical models were originally based, and with which they continue to be associated. As opposed to constructivist models, the behaviourist model depended largely on conditioning the learner to acquire and react to knowledge, and unsurprisingly met with resistance from feminist educators (see Whitehouse 2002).

The apparent disadvantages of older forms of DE thus appear evident: these may hinder experiential learning, inter-personal discussion, be overly dependent on technology and 'delivery' models, and create isolated, remote learning communities and 'passive consumers'. The more equitable partnership between teachers, students and peers, as envisioned in the feminist classroom, risks being re-mapped as the divorce between teachers and learners in the literal miles of distance invoked by DE. Knowledge, rather than being born within the confines of an intimate partnership, is represented as being summarily dropped off at the doorstep of the learner. In a survey published in 1990, Kirkup and Von Prummer noted that 'distance study can be a very socially isolated experience' and more of a problem for women. Perceived in its limited role of knowledge delivery to passive consumers, DE could very well run counter to feminist ethics of knowledge sharing as community building, and knowledge creation in equitable environments. Mohanty (2003) aptly expresses the feminist apprehension that DE 'shifts the focus from the actors in the educational process to the products (syllabi, lectures, etc.) of educational labour, which are then classified and marketed for profit' and that it portends the end of 'pedagogy as we know it' (180).

Further, the promotion of DE as a primary method of women's access to knowledge runs the risk of reinforcing gender stereotypes by confining women's educational access within domestic spaces. From the early 'missionary' character of correspondence courses which did little in terms of disturbing women's traditional roles in society (Larreamendy-Joerns and Leinhardt 2006, 573–574) to contemporary feminist acknowledgments of the dangers of using DE in ways which will end up 'perpetuating women's roles as primarily wives and mothers relegated to the domestic sphere' (Patterson 2009, 11), it is evident that DE has not always pursued a radical, liberatory path as far as women's social roles are concerned. Patterson's comment that 'distance education should be viewed as a temporary fix' (11) reflects a general feminist scepticism, just as much as Murray et al.'s caution that 'as feminists', we need to be wary of 'making ourselves complicit in maintaining women's relegation to the private sphere' (Murray Jessica and Koenig-Visagie 2013, 344).

Under these circumstances, is it possible to imagine a happy convergence between the two? Recent times have seen various feminist scholars engage with DE to set aside pre-existing biases, and recognise some of its affinities with feminist ethics. For instance, the 'delivery' metaphor, with its implied, patriarchally conceived passive, reproductive relationship, has been contrasted against the more participatory one of the mid-wife 'who facilitates the birth of what's already growing inside' (Chick and Hassel 2009, 203; see also Hipp 1997, 45). Feminist educators have also employed Freire's (1971) critique of the concept of 'banking' in education in similar efforts to resist such models (Rose 1995, 58; Von Prummer, Kirkup, and Spronk 1988, 59). As DE shifts emphasis away from knowledge delivery to knowledge construction through participatory learning, and embraces the 'openness' of ODL, the chasm between feminist ethics and DE becomes easier to traverse. Hipp observes that in the late 1990s, such pedagogical transformations in DE brought about a change in women students' level of apprehension in undertaking DE courses and enabled them to 'find their voices' (Hipp 1997, 44).

Specific learner-centric features of ODL pedagogy are also conducive to feminist praxes. At the very outset, one may note that while conventional instructional modes are referred to as f2f *teaching*, the ODL method focuses on distance *learning*, gainfully disrupting received notions of teacher-centric and learner-centric approaches. In a parallel to feminist pedagogy, distance learning material locates the learner at the centre of the teaching space. The conversational, interactive and lucid style of self-learning materials (SLMs) is intended to facilitate a critique of objectivist and authorless positions of textbook language (see Agger 1991, 122). It implies a tacit collaboration between the course material as teacher, the counsellor at the study centre as facilitator, and the learner as active participant, with peer groups at study centres functioning as 'classmates' for team-based activities.

In the early twenty-first century, the gap between DE and feminist pedagogy has been further reduced as feminist educators began exploring the 'transgressive influences of digital technologies' (Akins, Check, and Autumn 2004, 34). Borrowing from hooks' (1994) concept of transgressive education, Akins et al. underscore the resistant potential of technological space in re-inventing identities so that online spaces become 'lifelines' for women who can interact 'without recriminations, in nonauthoritarian settings' (45). It is becoming increasingly commonplace to acknowledge the potential of adapting technology to meet women's needs, and to view the virtual domain as a safer discourse space which may even offer subversive possibilities. Kendall (1998) identifies cyberspace as a safe zone for 'identity play and experimentation' (150). Maher and Huang Hoon (2008) see it as 'a more democratic terrain' in which 'students can . . . have their voices more freely heard' (204). The anonymity of virtual interactions may be liberating for some women; equally, non-traditional women who see themselves as anomalous on a college campus may feel more comfortable online (Kramarae 2001).

However, significant caveats have also been proffered against assuming the 'neutrality' of cyberspace as a given (Kirkup 1996; Kendall 1998; Von Prummer 2004; Murray Jessica and Koenig-Visagie 2013). Offline inequities (such as gender, race and class) may remain non-neutralised in the virtual world, calling attention to the need for an ongoing vigilance. In response, Richards (2011) advocates an 'ethics of care' (8) in the articulation of a 'cyberfeminist pedagogy' (6). Schweitzer (2001) views cyberspace as 'the greatest opportunity for feminism' (188) while qualifying that 'ultimately, this depends on one's attitude toward the Web's potential as a liberatory space' (204).

Cautionary notes notwithstanding, it must be acknowledged that online environments create an inclusivity which may level the playing field for women with physical disabilities, unemployed women, those with young children, or for women who cannot otherwise afford the money or time for getting an education. Chick and Hassel (2009) make a convincing case for an interface between the online environment and feminist pedagogy, asserting that they 'can and should be productively paired' (196) (see also Turpin 2007).

In what may seem like a throwback to Moore's notion of 'transactional distance', in recent years, cyber-ethnography has further helped to collapse the online/offline dichotomy in its growing assertions about the pervasive intrusion of the real and the virtual upon each other. If, as Daniels (2009) suggests, digital technologies are 'embedded in everyday life' (117) and internet practices reveal how women use these 'to improve, or at least change, the material conditions of their lives and their bodies' (111), early reservations against the implied distance of virtual technologies may lose their edge. Similar sentiments about the 'interspacial' aspects of virtual lives have been variously asserted – Ward (1999) posits hybrid spaces as enabling, claiming that 'the physical and the virtual envelop each other' (para 6.3); Rybas and Gajjala (2007) opine that 'being online and being offline are intersecting and interweaving experiences' (para 8) and Davies (2004) explores 'sustained interaction' in cyberspace as an integral part of 'ongoing lifetime conversations' for women (36). Calling the separation of real/virtual a 'false dichotomy' Leander and McKim (2003) emphasise how, in fact, these spaces are 'coarticulated' (212).

Further, the notion of digital literacies as 'placed resources' (Prinsloo and Rowsell 2012) has elucidated how technologies are 'shaped by context' and how ad hoc improvisations and novel uses of resources may lead to surprising possibilities (271–272). Arguing against the logic of 'digital divide' thinking, Prinsloo (2005) emphasises the 'socially situated nature' of technology (3). It is clear from the work of cyber-ethnographers that the virtual world may be 'experienced' in very 'real' ways, 'extending', rather than replacing, the real (see Leander and McKim 2003, 219). This has helped to relax the seemingly unyielding boundaries between the real and the virtual, already under investigation by feminist pedagogy.

All of these efforts further cement the gap between feminist pedagogy and ODL, allowing the former to focus on their shared social values, that is, inclusivity and democratisation. Larreamendy-Joerns and Leinhardt (2006) describe democratisation as 'increasing either the access to higher education of populations that would be otherwise excluded, or increasing the range of people who might be served by elite institutions' (575). This remains particularly true in developing countries where ODL continues to be perceived primarily as a public social experiment for inclusive, equitable educational access, unlike the west where it may become conflated with privatised, commercial enterprise.

Based on its defining ethic of reaching the unreached, ODL offers a particularly welcome alternative to women. Since time management remains a critical issue for many women burdened by domestic responsibilities, as well as for working women and men, online learning can function as a 'third shift' which, although unjust by its very definition, may enable an eventual escape from some of the burdens of the first and second shifts (leading to better working conditions, escape from domesticity, financial independence, ability to afford childcare, etc.). From the perspective of feminist pedagogy, however, it is important to flag that democratisation must be pursued not only at a *systemic level* through inclusive outreach, but equally at the level of *substantive transformations* – through a democratisation of ways of knowing and thinking, and a liberation from hegemonic ways of constructing knowledge. In this context, women's studies courses can play a significant role in reinforcing the democratising mandate of both ODL and feminist ethics, thus making them 'natural' allies. At the same time, feminist educators must remain alert to ODL's privileging of systemic democratisation over other forms. In the next section, these issues are addressed in the context of developing countries like India.

ODL and feminist pedagogy in developing countries

Distance learning theories established in the 1980s in the west[4] and the west-to-east drift of knowledge construction continue to determine ODL practices in India. In this regard, it is revealing to situate the current phase of DE in India on an international map. Patterson (2009) summarises the evolution of DE pedagogy in terms of three distinct stages – a first generation of correspondence teaching with sole reliance on print material in the early twentieth century, a second generation of multimedia aided education developed in the late 1960s, and finally a third generation of web-based technology enabled learning since the late twentieth century (3–4). However, the jump from first to third may not have been as smoothly accomplished in developing countries, where infrastructural constraints have hampered the large scale implementation of technology enabled pedagogies. Reports from different areas of the developing world evidence similar experiences. Murray, Byrne, and Koenig-Visagie's (2013) case study of gender studies at the University of South Africa indicates that until as recently as 2012, 'postal correspondence' (340) was the mainstay of curricular transaction and that the university is in the process of implementing online education to bring it 'in line with distance education providers globally' (340). The UNISA model parallels the current scenario in India, where behaviourist models continue to prevail over constructivist ones. In populous and economically strained nations, institutions are burdened with mass outreach to millions of students and shifts in established ways of functioning can be a slow, arduous and frustrating process. Consequently, the risk that enduring behaviourist pedagogies may reinforce gender hierarchies remains a real one.

As we have seen, online feminist instructional models in the west have successfully challenged the delivery aspect of DE through adaptations of technology, especially through a radical departure from previously held real/virtual dichotomies. However, these efforts are largely based on the assumption of an unrestricted tech-accessibility, except as noted by individual educators dealing with students in rural areas (see Rose 1995). In developing countries, virtual pedagogic praxis must confront not only constraints of access which vary across urban/rural and regional divides, but also consider that 'gender effects might be more marked', or at least differently marked, making women's 'participation in distance education even more difficult' (Von Prummer, Kirkup, and Spronk 1988, 57).

More significantly, higher education institutions in developing countries are particularly susceptible to consumerist pressures, which translate into a demand for high enrolment courses. In educational environments increasingly dominated by market exigencies, there is a fair deal of management of educational initiatives, especially those perceived as more vulnerable to economic considerations. Interestingly Kirkup and Whitelegg (2013) report similar experiences in the context of UK Open University's Women's & Gender Studies (WGSs) programmes which are under compulsion to demonstrate a 'positive contribution to the finances of the university' (15).

Such compulsions endanger the viability of 'special interest' limited enrolment programmes. This vulnerability is further underlined by the fact that knowledge generation may not be seen as a viable independent function of the institution and must be economically linked with appropriate tools of 'need assessment', 'cost analysis' and 'marketing strategies'. DE scholars have rightly cautioned against the dangers of choosing financial imperatives over socially beneficial pedagogical rationales. For instance, Larreamendy-Joerns and Leinhardt (2006) underscore the 'commodification argument' as an ongoing critique of DE (592) and Richards similarly critiques the 'fiduciary rationale' at the basis of DE courses (2011, 6).

On the other hand, ODL institutions, given their affirmative social mandate, cannot fail to recognise the significance of 'socially relevant' programmes such as WGS. This contradiction keeps alive a tension between economic compulsions and (lip service to) democratic ideals. It is foregrounded by administrative vacillations represented on the one hand, in a rhetoric of political correctness, and on the other, through interrogations of legitimacy. In the case of WGS courses, which tend to draw a 'niche' groups of students, the urgent insistence on cost effectiveness impedes the process of gradual percolation of ideas that may be a prerequisite for eventual shifts in cultural consciousness.

Overall, the partnership between feminist ethics and ODL obligations in developing countries is at once buoyed up by their shared democratic mandate and dragged down by economic compulsions, as evidenced through Women's Studies programmes which highlight this tension.

Managing women's studies at the ODL institution in India

The central (state owned) university (Indira Gandhi National Open University/IGNOU) where I currently work is the primary and pioneer provider of mass-based ODL education in the country, often touted as 'the largest university in the world' with presently over 2.81 million enrolled students (*IGNOU Profile* 2015, 4). Typically, ODL programmes attract a socially and economically diverse student population cutting across gender, age, class, caste and regional divides. One of the primary objectives of the university is to provide higher education access particularly for marginalised and disadvantaged groups, including women, differently abled and scheduled castes and tribes (*IGNOU Profile* 2015, 4). Founded on an explicit belief in inclusive education, the university has held firm in its emphasis on the primacy of ODL and summarily rejected a brief experiment with the conventional f2f mode which tends to be viewed as relatively exclusionist, if not elitist.[5]

The university ascribes to established DE pedagogical models (with printed course material along with multimedia as the mainstay of SLM) and is on the cusp of transitioning to online education. Prevailing models tend to be prescriptive in nature – course content follows a strict structure of blocks and units (roughly equivalent to books and chapters). Units are highly stratified and must contain an introduction, learning objectives, distributed content, text boxes for summary information, a 'Let Us Sum Up' section by way of conclusion, and 'Check Your Progress' questions at frequent intervals (with possible answers provided). The intractable nature of SLM structures derived from early models of 'programmed instruction' (Larreamendy-Joerns and Leinhardt 2006, 595)[6] implies that transaction tends to remain trapped in the 'delivery' model, leaving little space for constructivist modulations and may well prevent free engagement with feminist ethics.

Needless to say, any WGS programme must find ways to meet such challenges through a 'blending' of content-based and systemic interventions. The illustration of a blended-mode programme discussed below is intended as one possible exploration (rather than a universal model) of design and delivery innovations used to overcome particular constraints.

A programme-based illustration

Methodology

The discussion which follows is based on a postgraduate programme at IGNOU. I have attempted to substantiate relevant issues with the help of anonymised student comments. These have been garnered from three sources: (i) online forum posts (2013–2016), (ii) an e-mail Feedback Study I conducted (referred to below as FS 2016) and (iii) individual e-mails sent to me by students.

About the programme

The MA in Women's & Gender Studies (MAWGS) programme was launched nationwide in 2013. The programme was developed over a period of four years (2009–2013) by a team led by two Programme Coordinators[7] and an 'expert committee' which helped with the finalisation of programme design and course outlines. The title of the programme reflects an ongoing need to sustain the focus on women's issues while locating them within a larger framework of 'gender as a process' (Kirkup and Whitelegg 2013, 11). The programme is aimed at students (especially women and marginalised groups) with a Bachelor's degree in any discipline, and an interest in feminist theoretical perspectives and gender issues. A survey carried out in 2009 revealed that a majority of potential learners were keen to pursue a specialisation area for the Master's degree. Consequently, the first year curriculum provides a broad-based grounding in feminist theories and inter-disciplinary gender perspectives, with the option to exit with a postgraduate diploma. In the second year, students branch off into one of two available specialisation areas: 'Gender, Literature & Culture' or 'Women's Studies' (Figure 2.1).

From its very inception, the programme faced doubts about its potential 'success', commonly measured in terms of enrolment numbers. By the accepted institutional yardstick, it was initially considered

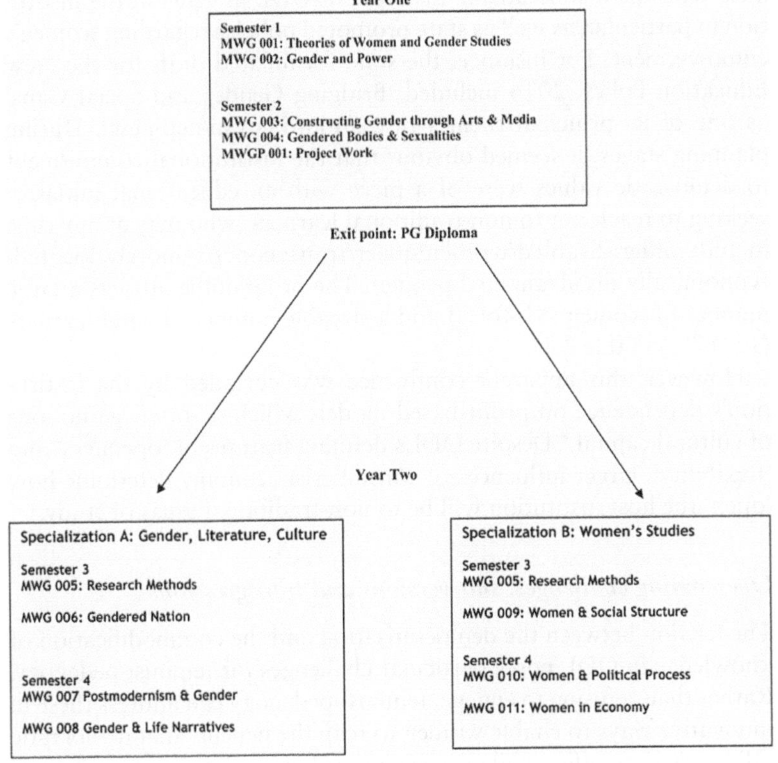

Figure 2.1 MAWGS: programme structure at a glance.

a 'low enrolment' programme and remained under surveillance, with the threat of closure always a potential reality (programmes with less than 100 fresh admissions annually are typically considered to be 'low enrolment'). It must be noted that such doubts regarding viability are not institution specific but are reflective of higher education's dominant fiduciary rationale as well as a general suspicion of gender studies – perceived as either not important enough to merit academic stature, or associated with limited interest groups (read, too radical or idiosyncratic). The relatively late appearance of Women's Studies on the institutional scene, and the suspicion of 'liberal, feminist agendas', continue to sustain such views. Fortunately, annual enrolments in the programme doubled in the first two years, with an increase from 69 in 2013 to 148 in 2015, laying to rest initial fears of sustainability (At the time of publication of this article, enrolments for 2016 have already crossed 165).

One aspect which worked in favour of the programme was its alliance with the democratising mandate of ODL in general, the institution in particular, as well as state promoted policies regarding women's empowerment. For instance, the state formulated draft for the New Education Policy, 2016 included 'Bridging Gender and Social Gaps' as one of its principal themes (http://mhrd.gov.in/nep-new). During planning stages, it seemed obvious that the institutional commitment to democratic values were of a piece with an educational initiative seeking to reach out to non-traditional learners (who may at any time include older/disabled/women/queer/transgender/remotely located/economically disadvantaged people). The programme attracts a large number of women (81–89%) and a sizeable number of rural learners (12–17%) (Table 2.1).

However, this apparent confluence was curtailed by the institution's dependence on profit-based models which de-privilege notions of cultural capital.[8] Despite ODL's defining features of 'openness' and 'flexibility', larger influences of consumerist economy determine how 'open' the host institution will be to non-traditional areas of study.

Overcoming challenges: sub-versions and transgressions

The friction between the democratisation and the commodification of knowledge in ODL poses particular challenges for feminist pedagogy. Rather than refusing to engage, feminist pedagogy can address these in innovative ways to enable women to reap the benefits that democratic ODL practices offer, while ensuring that feminist ethics are not compromised at the hands of consumerist ideology.

Table 2.1 MAWGS disaggregated data, 2014–2016.

Variable	*Total*	*Location*		
		Urban	*Rural*	*Unknown*
2013–2014				
Gender				
Women	59	53	6	–
%	85.5	89.83	10.16	
Men	10	8	2	–
%	14.49	80	20	
Total % of urban/rural learners		88	12	
Total (all learners)	69	61	8	
2014–2015				
Gender				
Women	71	60	7	4
%	88.75	84.5	9.85	5.63
Men	9	3	6	–
%	11.25	33.33	66.66	
Total % urban/rural learners		78.75	16.25	
Total (all learners)	80	63	13	4
2015–2016				
Gender				
Women	121	45	16	60
%	81.75	37.19	13.22	49.58
Men	27	12	5	10
%	18.24	44.44	18.51	37.03
Total % urban/rural learners		38.5	14.19	
Total (all learners)	148	57	21	70

At a time when consumerism holds sway, curious consequences emerge for feminist scholars engaged in the development of WGS programmes. Consumerist ideology's predilection for multiple options encourages a proliferation of 'choices' in a supermarket academic structure, what has elsewhere been termed as 'busy consumerism' (Agger 1991, 108). 'Choice' consequently operates as a code word for a surfeit of 'saleable' educational products, discouraging the consumer-learner from drifting away to another institution. The inherently flexible nature of the ODL system, with its facilitation of options, is particularly compatible with the consumerist thirst for 'choice'.

The progressive structure of the MAWGS programme with built-in options and specialisations[9] is seemingly in tandem with consumerist trends. However, for some students, the choice-based structure helped transform 'busy consumerism' into critical choices which matter, combining as it does, inter-disciplinary breadth (first year) with disciplinary rigour (second year). As reported by one student, 'unfortunately, fifteen years ago when I was in college, hardly any university offered such a programme in India' which now enabled her to pursue a specialisation for professional growth (FS 2016). A college teacher in a Commerce department (with a budding alternate career as feminist journalist), observed that the Women's Studies specialisation allowed her to enhance her 'writings for the local Dailies' and hoped that it would enable her to 'switch over to Women's Studies' one day (FS 2016); another felt that the 'specialisation is important' because 'one can choose the depth of any stream' after obtaining a 'comprehensive panoramic view across diverse topics, disciplines . . .' (FS 2016).

The institution's tacit approval of course design may not, however, be reflected in a parallel endorsement of course content and emerging disciplinary areas are often pressed to demonstrate their conformity to larger public agendas (see Wiegman 2002, 23). This implies that public institutions, while wedded to a progressive rhetoric, may be blocked from actualising such commitments due to perfunctory concerns with gender issues. ODL institutions may adhere to the democratisation mandate at a systemic level (educational outreach) but the substantive democratisation of knowledge represented by feminist pedagogy may not be equally welcome.

Many of the MAWGS courses provoke critical engagements with received knowledge systems, 'eye-openers' in the words of one learner (FS 2016). To undo the unyielding format of SLM, application-based assignments, exams which encourage analysis and creative expression, and a personalised internship/research project component which incorporates experiential aspects (see Agger 1991, 131) have been introduced. At the level of content, normative institutions, such as marriage, family and motherhood, are interrogated from a cross-cultural, feminist perspective. I have selected two e-mail responses which show how students continue to personally engage with issues they read about, often under difficult circumstances:

(i) Learner 1

As a political science student and before coming to know about feminism, I always thought that 'feminism is not good; it does not allow women to settle down in life; feminist always want to fight; they don't have routine life; good women are never feminists; the society looks down upon feminism and feminists . . . [they] always stand out and stand alone.

Much later I realised the reality was something else. And, I was v wrong in my understanding. The society around had taught me wrong and always discouraged me to get into this discourse, even at the level of reading a book on feminism or women rights. Later, I realised why . . . the society does not like to be questioned . . . the dominant norms like to preserve their norms . . . patriarchy enjoys support from majority . . . the minority that questions follows a tough path . . .

But, does reading help in any way. Till recently, I thought, 'Ignorance is bliss' and then one day my sister added, 'until u fall'. So, then I realised that . . . it does help to fight and question even if it is in silent and covert forms.

After marriage, I realised that woman's prime space of activity is kitchen. If she is not in kitchen, she is not doing anything. (I have resisted to be in kitchen 24*7, I get to hear many things, . . .)

Personal observations:

- woman does not have a home of her own – either fathers and husbands
- change of surname is a must (even though till date i am resisting it)
- the word 'sanskari' [traditional] is boundless . . . it is used as a justification and a method of control over women.
- During my pregnancy, all expected the baby to be a boy despite the fact that I explained the X-Y chromosome funda. And then, there were various predictions and superstitions. And, two months back when my daughter was born, I could feel their inner sadness. It was then for the first time i resented and questioned the behaviour and attitude of others. this also resulted in a heated discussion with my in laws.

(e-mail: June 23rd, 2016)

(ii) Learner 2

I believe that one of the greatest insights that the course material has offered is the ability to discern that gender roles, especially after marriage, are constructed. That one is socialised into these roles. . . . Doing the programme well has given me the confidence

> to combine academics with being a full time mother. I also ask my husband for a greater participation and sharing in domestic work & child care. The latter, I believe needs to be actively promoted in India.
>
> (e-mail: June 24th, 2016)

In MWG 001, 002, 007 and 008, concurrent discussions of race and caste, black feminism and *dalit* feminism, western 'fashion' and cultures of 'veiling', engage students in an ongoing transnational feminist dialogue between India and the globe, and with notions of entrenched gender, caste and religious inequities. One student commented that this 'deepened' her 'understanding of what it is to be a feminist in an otherwise unequal world' (FS 2016). Another commented that – 'understanding power or lack of it has deeply impacted me. So instead of struggling individually I can relate to the context personally as well as when I relate it to others' (FS 2016).

Some questioned whether or not western feminism could address the issues of oppressed *dalit* women in India. As suggested by one, 'feminism . . . must address inequality at the level of a value or ideology before we look at how it can help specific groups' (FS 2016). Contrarily, a student identifying as a 'global woman citizen' felt 'inclined towards rejecting postcolonial feminism' because she found it 'very difficult to relate to white feminists v. native feminists narrative anymore now that we are living in 21st century' (http://wgsforum.ignouonline.ac.in/wgforum/mawgsforum/ucp.php, 15 June 2015).

Particularly significant are transgressive perspectives on issues such as violence against women. While dominant, public discourses privilege notions of 'safety' over 'freedom' (especially as a permanent solution to violence and rape), circumscribing women's power within their domestic, familial roles as mothers and wives (rather than as single women), many of the course discussions resist such assumptions. 'Emancipation' and 'liberation' are explored through Indian and international women's movements and feminist theories (especially MWG 001). Patriarchally sanctioned violence against women is interrogated through a critique of normative definitions of masculinity (MWG 002). One student commented that while 'the State is going hammer and tongs against any form of dissent, rebellion or non-state discourse' we still do not have answers to the question – 'are women safe in our modern developed cities, in well lit and so called policed streets, at work place, leave alone the safety within homes?' (http://wgsforum.ignouonline.ac.in/wgforum/mawgsforum/ucp.php, 9 September 2013)

Several courses address the 'sensitive' subject of non-normative sexualities. In MWG 001 global queer and transgender movements are examined alongside problems of the *hijra* community in India. As observed by a student, the readings made him realise the importance of 'liberty not only for the women folk, but also for Queer/LGBTI community, Ghetto and Black liberalism' (http://wgsforum.ignouonline.ac.in/wgforum/mawgsforum/ucp.php, 12 October 2015). In a country where homosexuality is still not decriminalised, alternative perspectives allow students to link these broader issues to their personal lives and local contexts. One of them observed that he now saw feminism as 'a break away from traditional definitions of masculinity, of macho-ism, when all sexes can live, . . .' (http://wgsforum.ignouonline.ac.in/wgforum/mawgsforum/ucp.php, 6 October 2015). Raising a familiar aspect of ancient Hindu iconography, another stated that for him, the figure of the 'Ardhanaranari ("the half man-woman")' upheld contemporary notions of 'gender fluidity'. He found support for his claim in 'the recently concluded Durga Puja' celebrations in his hometown of Kolkata, where 'this concept' had been accorded 'status' (http://wgsforum.ignouonline.ac.in/wgforum/mawgsforum/ucp.php, 12 October 2015).

Exploring in-between spaces: a blended model

Systemic interventions in delivery modes are as necessary as content-based explorations for reconciling feminist pedagogy and ODL. Infrastructural constraints on offering a purely online programme in IGNOU impelled an experimentation with 'blending' online and prevalent DE modes. Here, Prinsloo's notion of 'placed resources' and ad hoc improvisations to maximise benefits from technology become particularly relevant since several restrictions had to be kept in mind when deciding the type of technology to be used. Due to limited student numbers in some areas, the programme could not be initially 'activated' at several study centres (the university normally mandates a minimum of 10 learners to make counselling services financially viable). This meant that learners at such locations were denied admission leading to a vicious cycle of low enrolments across the board. Another constraint was irregular access to technology and the varied profiles and locations of learners (rural/semi-urban/lower income urban households). Women's movements may be constricted due to gender biases, child-rearing responsibilities, religious, geographical or cultural constraints. Given that women's safety remains a daunting issue across the country, limitations on regular visits to the local internet café also had to be taken into account.

A study of an undergraduate programme in Computer Application at IGNOU shows women's limited access to ICT due to 'socio-cultural barriers' (Bhushan 2008, 131). A significant gendered technology gap was not, however, found in my 2015 survey of MAWGS students' access to internet facilities (Table 2.2). An overwhelming majority of learners (over 90%) confirmed ability to access internet facilities regularly from home (of the three students who did not have a computer at home, one had regular internet access on a smartphone – see Table 2.2). Still, irregular access as a result of infrastructural limitations, and rural/urban divides, continues to be a deterrent for some learners. A totally 'online' synchronous platform was not an ideal option since it implies that all students must be able to come online at

Table 2.2 MAWGS need assessment for online forum, 2015 survey (total number of respondents: 31).

1: Learner profile: age group					
Traditional (19–25 years, recently graduated)					7
Non-traditional (above 25 years)					24
Working	Student/non-working	Social worker	Stay at home mother	Unknown	
13	1	1	2	7	
2: Learner profile: gender					
Women = 24	Men = 7				
3: Access to Internet from computer device at home					
Yes[a]	No[b]			Total	
28 (90.3%)	3 (9.6%)			31	
4: Frequency of access to Internet from home[a]					
Daily (once/more than once)	Weekly (2/3 times a week)			Once a week	
20	3			5	
5: Access to Internet outside the home[b]					
Twice a week	Once a month			Only on phone	
1	1			1	

[a]No. 4 is a break-up of the 28 respondents who have access to Internet from home.
[b]No. 5 is a break-up of the three respondents who can only access Internet facilities outside the home.

scheduled times. This is further complicated by the working lifestyles of many of our students who come to DE primarily because of the learning pattern flexibility it promises.

In order to maximise ODL benefits to women and learners in remote areas, a dedicated, cost effective asynchronous online discussion forum was hosted on the institution's server in 2013, and has now been listed as a 'best practice' for ODL institutions in India.[10] It is intended to act as an additional support to learners, without supplanting the counselling sessions that they would normally attend at local study centres. Additionally, for learners who do not have access to counselling services, it functions as a means of personalised, qualitative communication with faculty and peers. Till date, this has been the primary rationale for dissuading regional centres from turning away eligible learners, regardless of location.

Students participate online at their convenience. The advantages of asynchronous, threaded dialogues as a way of promoting collaborative knowledge and greater participation have been noted by several feminists as well (Akins, Check, and Autumn 2004, 37; Maher and Huang Hoon 2008, 206; Lai and Lu 2009, 60–61). Moreover, the notion of 'transactional distance' which undoes the privileging of certain forms of 'dialogue' over others, along with cyber-ethnographers' assertions regarding the interpolation of online/offline spaces, help to validate such a blending of modes.

The forum has become the primary means of undermining the masculinised materialities of SLM through free discussion and debate on any of the topics studied. Course material can provide important tools for feminist research but analysis and critique are liable to become stultified due to the 'sage on the page' format. The forum acts as a way of extending knowledge beyond the printed page and students use it to exchange views and relate readings to current events. For instance, the much debated release of Leslee Udwin's 'India's Daughter' documentary (based on the infamous Nirbhaya gang rape and murder of a young girl in New Delhi in 2012) became a talking point on the forum in 2015. Students posted links to film reviews to justify their individual perspectives. The film's exposure of defence lawyers arguing in favour of the rapists led at least one student to express her rage online – 'lawyers express their so called "learned" views. One wonders are these guys cultured and educated? They re-echo obsolete patriarchal views and relegate women to the lowest rung in society'. She also wondered if 'education apart from dishing out degrees to such brutes' had 'done anything at all to transform them' (http://wgsforum.ignou-online.ac.in/wgforum/mawgsforum/ucp.php, 7 March 2015). Another student felt that 'the protests against Udwin's movie had proved that post-colonial feminism is still very much a thought' despite its conflict with 'nationalist patriarchy' which for her, stood for 'the far right wing's nationalist agenda to treat Hindu women as nation's property, holder of nation's honour and therefore a need to control their sexuality'. This, she felt was 'a challenge to us and an infringement of our right to choose our partners in love or sex' (http://wgsforum.ignouonline.ac.in/wgforum/mawgsforum/ucp.php, 15 June 2015).

Additionally, the online forum overcomes common infrastructural limitations. For the many students located in remote areas who fail to obtain SLM in time, it provides instant access to uploaded course materials, mirroring the experience of other feminist scholars teaching in rural areas across the world (similar experiences with postal delays have been reported by Burge and Lenskyi (1990) in rural Ontario). Unlike published material, virtual space allows for regular 'updation', drawing attention to the changing, fluid quality of information.[11]

Overall, virtual space enables an intimacy that SLM aspires towards. As Akins, Check, and Autumn (2004) observe, the Internet 'can feel and be less authoritarian and more intimate, possibly closer to the ways each of us asks life questions' (45). At least one student has regularly shared links to her own publications – poems, articles, illustrations and other creative work, while others post links to useful resources such as newspaper articles and film reviews. Participants engage with diverse opinions, enabling them to shift from a 'witness' to a 'participatory' space with the liberty to weave in and out of the two.[12]

In this regard, a limitation of the forum has been that in the absence of any 'real' contact (except with a few local students who drop by occasionally), it has been challenging to encourage greater online participation from those who prefer to remain silent 'lurkers' (e-mail reminders have shown limited success). Possible causes undoubtedly require future investigation even while considering that in many cases 'lurking' or online 'silence' may not necessarily signify non-participation (see Gajjala 2003; Leander and McKim 2003). In this particular programme, which draws a majority of women, gender identity certainly does not seem to be a major factor for non-participation. While one (female) student observed that 'in fact, I would feel my gender enables' participation (e-mail 23 June 2016), another comfortingly remarked that although, due to time constraints, she could not make 'use of [the forum] in the way it might have been ideally envisaged . . . with time the . . . evolution of the course as a meeting of minds and a sense of community will come' (FS 2016).

'Let Us (Not) Sum Up'!

The above phrase alludes ironically to the concluding section of a typical DE unit which accurately 'sums up' information. Flowing, ongoing interactions between feminist pedagogy and ODL lead us to conclude that the relationship is not easily summarised. Notwithstanding, we can surmise that their common democratising mandate continues to be the mainstay for reconciling differences internationally. Diverse means for achieving this must be innovated depending on the context. Shared pedagogical values and an exploration of productive 'hybrid' inter-spaces between real and virtual have alleviated misgivings about the suitability of ODL for feminist pedagogy in the west. In developing countries like India, the tension between the affirmative social function imagined for ODL and the challenges posed by increasing consumerist pressures, calls for specifically tailored responses. Here, the suggestive 'hybrid' metaphor needs to be blended to localised contexts, as exemplified through the discussion of one particular postgraduate programme. As on date, these efforts continue to bear promising results – steadily increasing enrolments, greater institutional support, and the activation of the programme at additional study centres across the country. As emphasised earlier, this illustration may have limited applicability in other contexts. It may, however, be indicative of the potential for building a strong, mutually productive alliance between feminist pedagogy and ODL across cultures.

Acknowledgements

I am indebted to Dr Nilima Srivastava, along with all other members of the programme team at the School of Gender & Development Studies for their contributions in the development and ongoing support of the MAWGS programme, to the Regional Services Division, IGNOU for providing relevant data related to this research, and to all the MAWGS students who provided important feedback for my research. I would also like to thank the two anonymous reviewers for their constructive comments, and Dr. Shubhangi Vaidya for her insightful reading of previous drafts of this article.

Notes

1 See Mohanty's (2003) elaboration of David Noble's phrase 'digital diploma mills'.
2 UK Open University: http://portal.unesco.org/education/en/ev.php-URL_ID=18650&URL_DO=DO_TOPIC&URL_SECTION=201.html

3 For distinctions between behaviorism, cognitivism and constructivism, see http://www. learningsolutionsmag.com/articles/301/how-do-people-learn-some-new-ideas-for-e-learning-designers
4 See Keegan (1997).
5 On campus mode was briefly introduced in 2011 and shut down in 2013.
6 For similar comments, see also Rose (1995), 54.
7 Programme Coordinators: Anu Aneja and Nilima Srivastava, School of Gender & Development Studies, IGNOU.
8 See Bourdieu (2011).
9 Based on a need assessment survey carried out in 2009; data analysis of survey done by Nilima Srivastava.
10 The MAWGS online forum has been listed as an example of "Best Practices in ODL" on a centralized site maintained by the University of Hyderabad: http://connect.uohyd.ac.in/cu-vcs-discussion-page/forum_topics/sharing-of-good-practices
11 Important updates such as the one regarding the December 2013 decision of the Supreme Court regarding Section 377 which overturned the previous (July 2009) High Court judgment de-criminalizing homosexuality have been a focal point of discussion.
12 I use these terms instead of the 'active/passive' binary since the witness space is not a passive one; it allows participants to be watchful, to assimilate without ostensibly participating.

References

Agger, Ben. 1991. "Critical Theory, Poststructuralism, Postmodernism: Their Sociological Relevance." *Annual Review of Sociology* 17: 105–131.

Akins, Future, Ed Check, and Rebecca Riley. 2004. "Technological Lifelines: Virtual Intimacies and Distance Learning." *Studies in Art Education* 46 (1): 34–47.

Bhushan, Poonam. 2008. "Connecting or Dividing? Examining Female Learners' Information and Communication Technology Access and Use in Open and Distance Learning." *Open Learning: The Journal of Open, Distance and e-Learning* 23 (2): 131–138.

Bourdieu, Pierre. 2011. "The Forms of Capital (1986)." In *Cultural Theory: An Anthology*, edited by Imre Szeman and Timothy Kaposy, 81–93. Oxford: Wiley-Blackwell.

Burge, Elizabeth, and Lenskyi, H. 1990. "Women Studying in Distance Education Issues and Principles." *International Journal of E-Learning &Distance Education* 5 (1): 20–37.

Chick, Nancy, and Holly Hassel. 2009. "Don't Hate Me Because I'm Virtual." *Feminist Teacher* 19 (3): 195–215.

Daniels, Jessie. 2009. "Rethinking Cyberfeminism(s): Race, Gender, and Embodiment." *Women's Studies Quarterly* 37 (1/2): 101–124.

Davies, Julia. 2004. "Negotiating Femininities Online." *Gender and Education* 16 (1): 35–49.

Freire, Paulo. 1971. *Pedagogy of the Oppressed*. Translated by Myra Bergman Ramos. New York: Herder and Herde.

Gajjala, Radhika. 2003. "South Asian Digital Diasporas and Cyberfeminist Webs: Negotiating Globalization, Nation, Gender and Information Technology Design." *Contemporary South Asia* 12 (1): 41–56.

Hipp, Helene. 1997. "Women Studying at a Distance: What Do they Need to Succeed?" *Open Learning: The Journal of Open, Distance and e-Learning* 12 (2): 41–49.

hooks, bell. 1994. *Teaching to Trangress: Education as the Practice of Freedom*. New York: Routledge.

IGNOU. 2015. *Foreword. Profile 2015*. New Delhi: IGNOU.

Keegan, D., ed. 1997. *Theoretical Principles of Distance Education*. New York: Routledge.

Kendall, Lori. 1998. "Meaning and Identity in 'Cyberspace': The Performance of Gender, Class, and Race Online." *Symbolic Interaction* 21 (2): 129–153.

Kirkup, Gill. 1996. "The Importance of Gender." In *Supporting the Learner in Open and Distance Learning*, edited by R. Mills and A. Tait, 146–165. London: Pitman.

Kirkup, Gill, and Christine Von Prummer. 1990. "Support and Connectedness: The Needs of Women Distance Education Students." *International Journal of E-Learning & Distance Education* 5 (2): 9–31.

Kirkup, Gill, and Elizabeth Whitelegg. 2013. "The Legacy and Impact of Open University Women's/Gender Studies: 30 Years On." *Gender & Education* 25 (1): 6–22.

Kramarae, Cheris. 2001. *The Third Shift: Women Learning Online. (Report)*. Washington, DC: American Association of University Women Educational Foundation.

Lai, Alice, and Lilly Lu. 2009. "Integrating Feminist Pedagogy with Online Teaching: Facilitating Critiques of Patriarchal Visual Culture." *Visual Culture & Gender* 4: 58–68.

Larreamendy-Joerns, Jorge, and Gaea Leinhardt. 2006. "Going the Distance with Online Education." *Review of Educational Research* 76 (4): 567–605.

Leander, Kevin M., and Kelly K. McKim. 2003. "Tracing the Everyday 'Sitings' of Adolescents on the Internet: A Strategic Adaptation of Ethnography Across Online and Offline Spaces." *Education, Communication & Information* 3 (2): 211–240.

Maher, Janemaree, and Chng Huang Hoon. 2008. "Gender, Space, and Discourse across Borders: Talking Gender in Cyberspace." *Feminist Teacher* 18 (3): 202–215.

Mohanty, Chandra T. 2003. "Privatized Citizenship, Corporate Academies, and Feminist Projects." In *Feminism Without Borders*, 169–189. London: Duke University Press.

Moore, Michael Grahame. 1997. "Theory of Transactional Distance." In *Theoretical Principles of Distance Education*, edited by D. Keegan, 22–38. New York: Routledge. Accessed 23 October 2015. http://www.c3l.uni-oldenburg.de/cde/found/moore93.pdf.

Moore, Michael Grahame. 2007. "The Theory of Transactional Distance." In *Handbook of Distance Education*, edited by M. Moore, 2nd ed., 89–105. Mahwah, NJ: Lawrence Erlbaum Associates.

Murray Jessica, Deirdre Byrne, and Leandra Koenig-Visagie. 2013. "Teaching Gender Studies Via Open and Distance Learning in South Africa." *Distance Education* 34 (3): 339–352.

Patterson, Natasha. 2009. "Distance Education: A Perspective from Women's Studies." *Thirdspace: A Journal of Feminist Theory & Culture* 9 (1): 1–16.

Prinsloo, Mastin. 2005. "The New Literacies as Placed Resources." *Perspectives in Education* 23 (4): 87–98.

Prinsloo, Mastin, and Jennifer Rowsell. 2012. "Digital Literacies as Placed Resources in the Globalized Periphery." *Language and Education* 26 (4): 271–277.

Richards, Rebecca S. 2011. "'I Could Have Told You *That* Wouldn't Work': Cyberfeminist Pedagogy in Action." *Feminist Teacher* 22 (1): 5–22.

Rose, Cronan. 1995. "'This Class Meets in Cyberspace': Women's Studies Via Distance Education." *Feminist Teacher* 9: 53–60.

Rybas, Natalia, and Radhika Gajjala. 2007. "Developing Cyberethnographic Research Methods for Understanding Digitally Mediated Identities." *Forum: Qualitative Social Research* 8 (3): Art. 35. http://nbn-resolving.de/urn:nbn:de:0114-fqs0703355.

Schweitzer, Ivy. 2001. "Women's Studies Online: Cyberfeminsm or Cyberhype?" *Women's Studies Quarterly* 29 (3/4): 187–217.

Turpin, Cherie Ann. 2007. "Feminist Praxis, Online Teaching, and the Urban Campus." *Feminist Teacher* 18 (1): 9–27.

Von Prummer, Christine. 2004. "Gender Issues and Learning Online." In *Learner support in Open, Distance and Online Learning Environments*, edited by Jane E. Brindley, Christine Walti, and Olaf Zawacki-Richter, 179–192. Oldenburg: University of Oldenburg, Center for Distance Education.

Von Prummer, Christine, Gill Kirkup, and Barbara Spronk. 1988. "Women in Distance Education." In *Developing Distance Education (Conference Proceedings)*, edited by David Sewart and John S. Daniel, 57–62. Oslo: Papers submitted to World Conference of International Council for Distance Education. Accessed 23 September 2015. www.files.eric.ed.gov/fulltext/ED320544.pdf.

Ward, Katie J. 1999. "The Cyber-Ethnographic (Re)Construction of Two Feminist Online Communities." *Sociological Research Online* 4 (1). Accessed 1 May 2016. www.socresonline.org.uk/4/1/ward.html.

Wiegman, Robyn. 2002. "Academic Feminism Against Itself." *NWSA Journal* 14 (2): 18–37.

Whitehouse, Pamela. 2002. "Women's Studies Online: An Oxymoron?" *Women's Studies Quarterly* 30 (3/4): 209–225.

3 Online education as 'vanguard' higher education

Exploring masculinities, ideologies, and gerontology

Lauren Ila Misiaszek

Background and introduction: unpacking 'less traditional' HE spaces

Understanding the particular pedagogical experiences of higher education (HE) instructors in for-profit universities, both online and traditional brick and mortar, is complicated but highly relevant. The sheer number of students that these instructors are serving is an indication of this importance. For example, the largest postsecondary institution in the US is the for-profit University of Phoenix, Online Campus, with over 307,000 students (over four times any other single university) (US Department of Education 2013). The second largest university in the US is the for-profit Ashford University with over 74,000 students (US Department of Education). Both universities have online and, to a lesser extent, campus degree programmes. In Fall 2011, online enrolment accounted for nearly 32% of students of all US degree-granting postsecondary institutions (Online Learning Consortium 2012). Only 12% of these institutions did not have any online offerings in 2012. In addition, nearly 63% of HE institutions now provide complete online programmes (Online Learning Consortium). I pause here to note that there are differences between 'online' and 'distance' education; in this article, 'online' will be (not unproblematically) operationalised as synonymous with 'distance education', in the same way it is operationalised by various actors above.

For-profit schools differ from their non-profit public and private counterparts in that 'while public and private non-profit schools aim to balance expenditures and revenues, private for-profit schools pay dividends to shareholders' (Hansen 2015). Many inequalities surrounding for-profits are quite commonly known: for-profits heavily recruit low-income students and Students of Colour (Hansen), student debt is higher (Hansen), and graduation rates are significantly lower – the six-year for-profit graduation rate is 20.4% compared to 55.7% (public) and 65.1% (private non-profit) (National Center for Education Statistics 2009 in Hansen 2015). Ashford, from the paragraph above, is affiliated with Bridgepoint Education, which has been in the middle of controversy over 'student retention, resource allocation and internal reviews' (Brown 2012). And while there is not space to discuss further quality or prestige issues of for-profits here, clearly these (deeply concerning) issues have more recently become highly visible.

In addition to the complexities of for-profit universities at the system level, part-time teachers' experiences (in both non-profit and for-profit settings) is also highly nuanced. Part-time teachers account for over 76% of all college instructors in the US – over one million instructors (Sanchez 2014). The inequalities that part-time teachers face are well known:

> Schools save money when they replace full-time, tenured faculty with itinerant teachers, better known as adjuncts. And a congressional report out today says that shift has created lots of tension on campus where adjuncts are treated like cheap labour.
>
> (Sanchez 2014)

Demographics about one of this group's subsections – *online* part-time instructors – are just beginning to be gathered, including the amount of teaching they do and the reasons for teaching part-time online (Starcher 2014).

The combinations of these categorisations of for-profit institutions are numerous, including combinations of course medium (e.g. traditional, web-facilitated, hybrid/blended, online), position type (e.g. to use the case of the US, tenured, tenure-track, non-tenured, adjunct, to use the case of the US), and contract type (e.g. full-time, part-time, contracted). Among the many financial issues, there are retirement concerns of part-time teaching. When the teacher is 65 or older, thus making her/him part of the largest-growing segment of US society (American Psychological Association, 2015), work in older age adds additional complexities in regards to part-time teaching, pay, and benefits. While, of course, these categorisations are not exhaustive, they introduce the range of aspects that make this analysis challenging.

Drawing inspiration from Sue Clegg's (2008, 241) statement that 'less traditional universities and areas of course provision and research might be important sites to investigate in relation to academic identity', I undertake a single strategic case study of an expert, older, male critical educator. I define 'expert' as someone who has devoted a significant amount of their professional trajectory to a specific aim, in this case, critical education, particularly the work of Paulo Freire; as will become evident, in this case this has involved obtaining a Ph.D. in the field. Doug S. (a pseudonym) is employed as a part-time instructor in two 'less traditional', for-profit settings: a solely online university and a brick and mortar university. I argue that it is particularly important to not arbitrarily isolate these two pedagogical settings, but instead examine their convergences and divergences, since the statistics above (and Doug's responses) highlight that these contexts often necessarily result in teaching and working in both. Since these universities, by their very nature, are designed to generate profit, and because they face the above-mentioned issues, these settings appear to position critical and feminist pedagogues in the proverbial 'belly of the beast'. In this paper, I ask the central research question, *how does a critical pedagogue navigate these 'less traditional' higher education settings?*

In the sections that follow, I first outline the theoretical starting point for this paper – a consideration of the future directions of the study of masculinities in education, masculinities online, and critical feminist gerontology, as well as a brief reflection about the role of Freirean studies (theoretical, methodological, and pedagogical work that reinvents that of Brazilian educator Paulo Freire). Then, I discuss the methodological rationale for the case study and its data collection, analysis, and presentation of data in the form of four 'sketches'. These four sketches focus on the following themes: autobiography; identity and pedagogy; ideology; and the future of these educational settings. I conclude with a discussion of the implications of this project for administrators, teachers, and students in these settings.

Theoretical framework: convergences of *inéditos viáveis*

There are endless ways to combine social identifiers into new 'gaps' in the literature, attempting to create what could feel to some readers as a 'niche' intersection and quite reductionist. For example, in this article, the intersection could be 'how older critical educators experience masculinities in online pedagogical spaces'. Despite this possible 'niche' risk, it is important to note that masculinities, ideologies, age, and online identity emerged as key, but not the only, liminalities in the research. Haywood and Mac an Ghaill explained how they arrive at liminalities as a useful construct:

> This post-structural emphasis on simultaneity can be identified in Youdell's (2010) exploration of pedagogy and boys with 'social,

> emotional and behavioural difficulties'. Rather than deploy social and cultural categories as intersecting, the use of simultaneity facilitates a conceptual liminality. This liminality is a position that is 'necessarily ambiguous, since this condition and these persons elude or slip through the network of classifications that normally locate states and positions in cultural space (Turner 1969, 95)'.
>
> (Haywood & Mac an Ghaill, 2012, 588)

This case study research is based on 'sketches' of these liminalities that could potentially be addressed by the convergence of future directions of the following three subfields: masculinities and HE from critical and feminist perspectives (Clegg 2008; Burke 2011; Haywood & Mac an Ghaill 2012); masculinities (and other identities) online (through the Internet research subfield of gender and technology) (Kendall 2011); and masculinities and aging from a critical, feminist gerontological perspective (Freixas, Luque, and Reina 2012).

By focusing specifically on scholars' visions of future directions for these subfields, I – and I argue, this scholarship – engage in the Freirean practice of considering the *inédito viável*,

> a process which assumes that by rethinking our past, we can fundamentally gain an understanding of the formation of our own self, the roots of our present condition, and the limits as well as the possibilities of our being a self-in-the-world.
>
> (Torres 2007, 158)

The *inédito viável*, 'that which has not yet been realized', is characterised by the concepts of *incompleteness, inconclusion, and unaccomplishedness* (Romão 2007). In the paragraphs that follow, I explore passages of *inéditos viáveis* from each of the fields, in an attempt to use these future directions as a starting point to examine the fields' convergences, which serve as a frame for the presentation of the study.

Masculinity and education scholars Chris Haywood and Máirtín Mac an Ghaill (2012) considered Britzman's idea of 'unthought' as it relates to understanding gender:

> . . . We might begin to think through the possibility of understanding gender that is not constituted by masculinity. This is perhaps the most conceptually and methodologically challenging approach. Asking the question of what is next for research on masculinity in education requires more than an engagement with approaches that conceptualise masculinities, it requires us to focus

> on 'not the ontological claims of identity, but the conceptualization made possible precisely because of what is unthought'.
>
> (Britzman 1997, 36) (589)

I argue that this 'unthought' is an expression of the *inédito viável.*

Scholar of masculinities online, Lori Kendall (2011), encouraged a push beyond the study of how identity is performed online towards a broader societal examination of the role of identity and new media:

> . . . We also need studies that push beyond such questions as, for instance, whether gender matters online (of course it does), and whether online gender performances reify or call into question existing hegemonic conceptions of gender. (Some do one, some the other, but why? And in what circumstances?) We also need studies that take a broader look at how the Internet and related media technologies intersect with our conceptions of identity and our very sense of self. Are, for instance, changes occurring in how we conceive of gender, of what gender means in society, and of the gendered balance of power? If so, what role do new media play? If not, why do the new forms of sociality afforded by new media not effect such changes?
>
> (322)

I argue here that Kendall's questions are useful here as they nuance discussions of the boundaries – the *inéditos viáveis* – of her field.

Finally, critical feminist gerontologists Anna Freixas, Bárbara Luque, and Amalia Reina (2012) particularly focused on bringing out the diversity of experiences of elderly women:

> Critical feminist gerontology has documented the experience of elderly women encouraging the development of more complete and more complex interpretations of their lives, and has discussed the necessity of studying and understanding the life trajectories in greater detail, revising the lacunae and inconsistencies that a large proportion of current gerontological studies offer, as a victim of the 'ideology of age' (Fine 1992) . . . The complex and subtle life of elderly women would appear to be a wide field, open to thinking and critical and reflective research, in which their voices and experience are revealed to be essential tools. The objective of such studies of the age of women should be to encourage the freedom of elderly women to choose their own lifestyle and the manner of aging that they prefer.
>
> (56)

I argue that the connections of this 'wide field' to other fields are only beginning to be explored outside of gerontological circles (for instance, this is a largely unexplored discourse in my field of comparative education), including its potential contributions across the lifespan and in analyses of men.

What is notable in these three excerpts about these fields' futures is that the priority discourses, while overlapping at times, respond to diverse concrete, material issues (issues that move beyond the theoretical to affect the real lives of people). Particularly, the way identity and gender are understood varies in each field. However, I would argue here that there is immense untapped potential for these highly established fields to symbiotically learn with and from each other. These converging *inéditos viáveis* frame this analysis.

Finally, as the employment of Freirean language here has already shown, Freirean studies are central in this paper's framework. The designation of 'studies' is not intended to apply that it is its own discipline – I am rather using it for purposes of readability; it is an overlapping focus of study across many fields. Introducing it here, in this section's conclusion, may appear as somewhat of a 'tacked on' afterthought. So it is important to make explicit that Freirean studies has significantly informed each of these three subfields in particular ways as well as my own thinking about these subfields (which I will touch on later in the paper). Yet, or perhaps because of this, the 'reinvention' of Freire's work can feel quite recycled at times to expert Freirean educators. Thus, perhaps the ways in which expert Freirean educators respond to 'less traditional' educational settings throughout their lifespans will be of interest to expert Freireans, and open dialogues about Freireans in distance learning and throughout the lifespan. It is the hope that this case may inspire new imagined futures of Freirean studies as well.

Methodology: illuminating a single case through 'sketches'

This is a two-part strategic case study of an expert educator in two 'less traditional universities' (Clegg 2008):

Part 1

For my 2012–2013 Fulbright research project, I conducted an expansion project of the UK's 2010–2012 Higher Education Academy National Teaching Fellowship Scheme Project, 'Formations of Gender and Higher Education Pedagogies' (GaP), a highly layered and participatory study focused on the development of inclusive HE pedagogies. (Burke et al. 2013). My research consisted of carrying out 9 focus groups with 44 HE academic staff in 4 countries – Portugal, Spain, Italy, and the US. The participants were recruited from an international research network focused on education and social justice. Participants were asked about the following issues: strategies, inequalities, and autonomy as it related to their teaching; how their teaching related to their other work in HE; and opportunities to challenge structures, policies or practices that negatively affected their teaching and/or relationships with students. Doug participated in the US focus group. At 68, he was the oldest male participant in the focus group, and the second oldest participant overall. I was drawn to the way in which his particular contributions illuminated some of the issues raised in the previously described framework that I had not considered before. A case study of a small number of particular participant(s) from critical and feminist perspectives is significant. Burke (2011, 176) clearly explained the logic of doing so:

> . . . I have selected two of the men's accounts to focus on, in order to provide a more detailed analysis of the processes of subjective construction in an individual's account of accessing higher education and experiencing migration. My purpose is not to draw attention to and reduce my analysis to a set of common themes running across the whole data set. Rather I want to look at the richness of the two men's accounts, both to theorise processes of subjective construction, as well as to problematise discourses of WP and to understand the ways the men categorised as 'home' students, have a range of other contradictory subjectivities, notably shaped by diasporic experiences, which form their self-understandings as students.

Bearing these aims and justifications in mind, I drafted a paper based on coding of Doug's excerpts from the focus group.

Part II

Sixteen months later, I conducted a follow-up interview to discuss this draft with Doug. This interview was audio-recorded, transcribed, and analysed using NVivo software. Twenty-one codes were produced, with 57 occurrences. Sketches, a concept that I will introduce below, were developed from a larger categorisation of these codes.

This additional interview could be considered somewhat of an expert 'member check' as Doug, as a holder of a Ph.D. in the field of critical education, can be considered an expert on this study's theory and methodology. Yet, I argue that it is beyond a 'member check' in that it was grounded in the sense that the purpose of the interview was not just to confirm his statements from the focus group but instead to use these statements to further explore his experiences. Thus, the methodology moved from the focus groups' bigger brush strokes of how he experienced autonomy, for example, to the interview filling in these broader brush strokes with the finer details about his particular identity and setting that were not initially explored. I found that beginning with these larger themes instead of with the particularities of his professional role(s) led to a more holistic picture being painted.

Methodological strategy of sketches

What follows is a series of four (what I am calling) *sketches* that draw on the data from Part I and II in order to explore how Doug navigates these 'less traditional' spaces. I have chosen to play with the methodological strategy of a *sketch* inspired by Stephen Ball's (2012) utilisation of *workbook* to describe one of his recent books, which begins with a foreword entitled '(Not) reading this book':

> First, the book is in part a workbook. It is an attempt to develop a method of policy analysis fitted to the current context of global education policy. A lot of things are being tried out for size. Some of the ideas or analyses you may think do not work or could be done differently. That is fine! I hope you will decide to take on some of the approaches outlined and take them further.
>
> (xii)

The precedent of this discoursal comfort in the inevitable discomfort of 'try[ing] [things] out for size', again brings to mind the central characteristics of the *inédito viável* (incompleteness, inconclusiveness, and unaccomplishedness). So while the space here does not allow for a 'workbook', per se, I am approaching these sketches with these same intentions.

Interestingly, the English word *sketch* traces its origins to the Italian word *schizzo* (of whose meanings include *splash*), which is appropriate as these sketches ask the reader to 'dive' into the subsequent sections of this paper. A sketch can be 'a rough drawing representing the chief features of an object or scene and often made as a preliminary study', 'a tentative draft (as for a literary work)', 'a brief description (as of a person) or outline', 'a short literary composition somewhat resembling the short story and the essay but intentionally slight in treatment, discursive in style, and familiar in tone', or 'a slight theatrical piece having a single scene; *especially*: a comic variety act' (Merriam-Webster.com). These first four definitions are each subtly different from each other and each brings out specific nuanced characteristics of these sketches. The last definition calls into attention the element of humour in Doug's accounts (which, at times, are quite confessional). Humour is certainly an important navigation tool in HE classrooms, often cited as important, but well-executed much less often. Hooks (2010) noted:

> I hope future efforts by educators to redefine learning will include discussions of ways to use humour productively in the classroom. We all know the kinds of negative humour that estrange people from one another. . . . We are not as familiar with the healing power of humour . . . All teachers could use more studies about sharing the power of humour as a force in the classroom that enhances learning and helps to create and sustain bonds of community. Working together in the classroom, teachers and students find equanimity when we laugh together.
>
> (74–75)

The connection of humour to the concept of a 'sketch' is an interesting one and there were moments in Doug's accounts in which he employed humour reflexively. Instead of placing Doug's simplified demographics in the methodology section, I have chosen to give them space of their own in this first sketch. Humour is not absent here but nor is it separated from more difficult issues in the discussion.

Sketches: writing towards the *inédito viável*

Sketch 1: auto/biography

In this sketch, the longest of the four, the reader is given a glimpse into Doug's highly nuanced understanding of himself through his responses to my demographic questions. Instead of reducing them into a single sentence, I have attempted to bring them to life as an illustration of the concrete roots of the analysis' theoretical convergences. I purposely guide the reader here through other social identifiers before arriving at the specific identifier – Doug's professional identity as a for-profit teacher; this sketch highlights how challenging it is to try to make sense of the personal and professional worlds of a 'for-profit' teacher (or any teacher for that matter).

After giving his age, which classifies him as an 'older adult' by most indicators, Doug reflected:

> It's an illusion; it's a number. I don't feel seventy. And I don't know what it is to feel seventy. I feel that I have the experience, strength and hope to go on for another 20, 25 years. Whether or not that's possible for me. I try to keep my body and soul in one place together. I feel good. I work out. I do my walking and my singing, you know, and my acting. I have the choice of end of life careers.

Of note here is Doug's envisioning of 20–25 more years of life and his 'end of life careers'. In his response to gender, his dry and reflective humour was apparent: 'Gender? Male. Unfortunately. Going to come back if there is a metempsychosis [transmigration of the soul, especially its reincarnation after death], as a female next time'.

When asked about his racial identity, Doug responded,

> I am a *Mischlingskinder* which is the Nazi definition of a 'mixed blood'. I am mixed kinder child, a mixed child, a mixed blood, which means that my father was a non-practicing German Jew brought up as a socialist. And my mother was of the Danish, Irish, French and probably Native American descent. And, they met, and I was the product of that marriage, the only one that survived. Therefore, I identify with no particular racial or ethnic group. Really I was, if given my own brothers, I would be, or I am by nature and training and *afición* [fondness/love], I am a *mulato*.

The gerontological understanding of *reminiscence*, 'the recall of personally experienced episodes from one's past' (Webster, Bohlmeijer, & Westerhof 2010, 528), particularly reminiscence for the functions of (discussing) identity and of teaching/informing (533), feels like an illuminating tool with which to explore this description. I argue that Doug engages in a *critical* reminiscence on work, gender, and race and ethnicity, drawing on his background in critical education as he reflects on his life. I further contend that the process of reminiscence, as well as the announcement of possible or imagined futures – *inéditos viaveis* ('hope to go on for another 20, 25 years', 'going to come back . . . as a female', 'if given my own brothers, I would be') – is both corporal and grounded in traditional social identifiers and, at the same time, transcends these identifiers since, to draw on Doug's ontological perspective, the future of that socially identified body is unknown. Confronting his potentially 'post masculine' future, Doug engages in (self) 'healing' humour in the hooksian sense around gender. Here, the words of Alanis Morissette and Guy Sigsworth (2008) song "Incomplete" seem apropos to this intersectionality of end of life, healing/humour, and the incompleteness of the *inédito viável.*

As well, the description brings to mind the Latin American concept of *testimonio*, 'the explicitly political narrative that describes and resists oppression' (Beverley 2000 and Tierney 2000 in Chase, 2010, 209) – provocatively re/claiming the oppressive label of *mischlingskinder* later in life. Doug's evocation of German and Spanish language draws on these traditions, on his multilingualism, and on his long history of experiences in Latin America, which I will return to in a moment.

These same concepts are relevant to his understanding of other social identifiers. The way in which he positioned himself geographically and how this relates to migration was also a key discussion because:

> I would like you to say that I am an immigrant. That I feel like an immigrant from Manhattan, which was an immigrant city when I left it. And that I came to this city [Los Angeles (LA)] 32 years ago . . . There are many Americas, but there is one America which is coastal or bicoastal. I am a product of the bi-coastal system.

In what I argue is an example of 'intergenerational intelligence' (Biggs, Haapala, and Lowenstein 2011) and 'intergenerational solidarity' (Biggs 2008). Doug connected his own experiences of his and his family's migrations to those of his students:

> But the family stories are the root of all. I don't bring this stuff up because I'm trying to get you off the subject. The family story is the root of it. Because absolutely when we end up in the desert of not knowing where to go next, what do we fall back on? Our family traditions, our training. And what scares me about this generation that I'm teaching either by remote control or in person is that their rootedness is sometimes all they have. Their rootedness is full of all kinds of what I would say striated, striated with addiction and abandonment, and so much of the struggle of trying to make, gain a foot hold in America and the pressures and what the pressures manifest. How the pressures manifest.

In addition to fluidly making connections about his personal history, Doug also moved fluidly across disciplines and languages, his formal education illustrating fluidity between humanities and social sciences disciplines. In his twenties, having completed Peace Corps service in Brazil, he obtained a BA in English literature from an Ivy League university. In his 50s, he obtained an MA in Latin American Studies from a prestigious public US university, and, in his early 60s, he completed a Ph.D. in Education from this same university. Before, during, and after obtaining these degrees, Doug's professional identities have shown great breadth and depth. He is an expert teacher, with over 40 years of experience in K-12, HE, adult education, and popular education. He is also a lifelong actor:

> . . . I was an actor when I came out here [to LA]. I came out here to play a part and audition. I got the part. I had a career. I have a pension from SAG [Screen Actors Guild]. I am getting back into it in my own old age in certain strange ways.

In addition, he is a writer, poet, professional Portuguese and Spanish translator, co-founder of an international social justice institute focused on Freirean Studies, and co-owner and manager (with his wife) of an international boarding house that has hosted over 100 international students and faculty.

Returning to this paper's introduction, highlighted among these professional identities is that Doug is currently an instructor in two for-profit educational settings. The first of the two settings is 'Pine University', a US online ('cyber', to use Doug's words) for-profit university with nearly 50,000 students. It is part of a network owned and operated by an educational company that also owns over 75 other universities in 30 countries with over 800,000 students. Doug has worked at Pine since 2008 and is currently a mentor–assessor for the university's educational leadership Ph.D. programme, a role that he describes as 'part instructor and part counsellor'. He supports students in their coursework via phone, email, and Blackboard. Here, Doug described the demographics of his students:

> I would say three quarters of my students are women, teachers, maybe more than three quarters. All but really – I've had 2 men in the last 5 years. All the rest have been women. Mostly middle-aged, middle age to seniors, all school teachers, public school teachers for the most part. I would say three quarters [are] Afro-American and wanting to get out of the classroom and become

> administrators and thinking that getting a PhD in Educational Leadership would be the key to that.

Before becoming a mentor–assessor, describing his previous experience at Pine, Doug noted,

> I have taught one or two classes there and found them not much to my liking because you don't have any autonomy. There's no, you have no, the classes are already laid out, the curriculum is established. Basically what you are doing is just correcting, reading and correcting and marking. And, you know, it's a lot of work. And not that gratifying because you don't have any creative bandwidth.

Our conversation about Pine echoed the negative issues that many for-profit university students face in terms of debt and graduation, as discussed in this paper's introduction:

Me: It does, in fact, that one of the whole themes that you brought out during the focus group discussion about some of the stories of your students in crisis.
Doug: In crisis, constant crisis.
. . . .
Me: You talked a lot about the debts and other experiences with the students. You bought them computers, etcetera.
Doug: One of them, I bought a computer for one of them who dropped. Most of mine, I have lost. . . . I have been in that university since 2008. . . . And I have yet to have the pleasure of hooding one of my mentees. But in terms of debt there are all in the 80 to 100,000 dollars plus category.

The second of these two settings is 'Oak University', a (private) for-profit brick and mortar 'professional training school' (to quote Doug) in Southern California. It is part of a larger system in the US and Canada of about 50 colleges with over 70,000 students. For the past few years, Doug has taught two courses at Oak: undergraduate courses on sociology and effective speaking. He teaches a large number of young immigrant students.

When asked about the impact of having courses to teach each semester at Oak, Doug reflected on the importance of these fluid professional identities:

> It's not going to crush me or kill me because I am not, my life isn't shaped that way so that I am super dependent on one thing. It

> hasn't been ever since I became – I learned as an actor. Have two or three things going – always. So that when one fades or disappears than the other will be enough to shore you up.

Ideologically, he also reveals that he considers himself to be a Freirean educator. His dissertation was focused on the history and legacy of Freire in northern Brazil.

In terms of class, Doug identifies often, and publicly, as a member of the 'working class-elite', which I felt was appropriate to mention after the other identifiers, because of the light they shed on this particular identifier.

In terms of our overlapping positionalities, Doug and I share the common interest in Freirean studies (we first met in 2006 through our work in this Freirean institute, and see each other several times a year). As well, we have academic and professional identities related to Spanish and Portuguese Language and Literatures. Doug has a 40-year head start on me in all of these fields. Also, notable here is that my interest in the field of critical gerontology emerged though my three years of full-time professional work in the field of geriatric and gerontological education and research (a field that is not related to my Ph.D.).

To illustrate some of the elements of this sketch, it is worth bringing up one critical conjuncture of this case: the first moments of our interview. When I arrived for the interview, Doug chose to present me with four documents: (1) a poem by (Brazilian singer, songwriter, playwright, writer, and poet) Chico Buraque in Portuguese, (2) Doug's own piece of original prose in Portuguese about his time as a Peace Corps volunteer in northern Brazil in the mid-1960s, (3) Nancy Scheper-Hughes's 1992 piece on 'Critical consciousness: The Method of Paulo Freire' in her 1992 book, *Death without Weeping: the Violence of Everyday Life in Brazil*; and (4) a recent personal email communication related to his online mentor–assessor role. This critical conjuncture offers one glimpse into the rich and myriad traditions of poetry, original prose, critical psychology, and pedagogical reflection via new media through which Doug makes meaning about and uses as tools to thrive within the spaces in which he works. The former three are unique tools of reminiscence (intimately connected to auto/biography), particularly reminiscence's teaching/informing function (Webster, Bohlmeijer, & Westerhof 2010, 533); the latter is a physical artefact from the virtual realm in which Doug is currently working to make sense of this moment in his lifespan/auto/biography.

Sketch 2: identity and pedagogy

In this sketch, Doug discussed how he conducts class, tightly interweaving reflections on his own identity. The first excerpt illustrates the challenges of renegotiating masculinities online:

> The cyber university challenges the teacher because you have to create a voice without ever, or very little, speaking, so you have to create a kind of online presence. And I found that extremely interesting as a challenge because . . . I'm a personality teacher, I'm an actor, I don't have any problem walking into classrooms and have not for the last 40-some years that I've been doing it and taking charge of a classroom which – like it or not – is the first thing that has to happen. The first thing that has to happen in a classroom is that people recognize that you are the instructor and doing that without presence and without voice, for me, was challenging. So what I saw it then as was kind of a literary exercise in creating a personality somewhat like mine but quite different, as it turned out, that then they would respond to as 'Dr. S' (his last name). Ok, so my character, and has been now for the last 5 years, is this person Dr. S who is a very, very interesting person. Very different from this (signals himself) person. Ok, a projection of me into a realm of non-presencial education, so that has been challenging.

Doug's statements that 'I don't have any problem walking into classrooms', 'taking charge', and 'people [have to] recognize that you are the teacher' illustrate how he exerts himself in the classroom. They align with traditional notions of gender and masculine performativity in relationship to teaching – ease, comfort, confidence, and 'natural' leadership. However, this online experience seems to point to vulnerability in terms of subjectivity/identity in online settings due to loss of overt ways of performing masculinity in presencial settings. Doug's description of the experience of being 'without presence' and 'without voice' points to a disruption in this traditional masculine, embodied performance; to address this loss of power – this new fragility – 'Dr S' was created.

The description of 'Dr S' signals a switch to the third person, suggesting Doug momentarily examined this situation from a different perspective. He goes on to reflect on age and gender in the online setting:

> [My online personality is] more avuncular. More *éminence grise*. . . . More understanding. Much more knowledgeable than

> I think I am in person. Solving problems not with ease but very, very encompassing. In other words, he's not only an instructor – because I'm not really, I'm a mentor-assessor – so I'm somewhere between a psychologist and your uncle that you always loved but never saw enough of.

A momentary slip back into the third person is of note here for its slight shift in manner of reflection. And his descriptions of his online persona as both (the gendered) *avuncular* and as an *eminence grise* illustrate the complexities of these new subjectivities and how they are performed. Doug has created a virtual self that is a more-ideal self.

As well, the excerpt highlights a pyscho/emotional relationship between Dr S and his students, which brings to mind Hey and Leathwood's (2009) discussion of the relationship between emotion and employability:

> The policy production of the 'employable' subject also implicates the affective from another direction. There are indications that professional and managerial work increasingly relies on 'emotional literacy' or 'emotional intelligence' (Gardner 1983; Groves et al. 2008). Being a competent professional establishes new norms for the ethical conduct of the 'in-touch' subject (be they academic managers or students and thus future employees) within the domain of higher education.
>
> (104)

The removal of 'corporality' in online pedagogical settings presents particular challenges to the concepts of 'emotional literacy' and 'emotional intelligence'.

The timing of *when* to connect with the student and the performativity surrounding this connection also stands out in this longer narrative of Doug's:

> It's kinda pulling a rabbit out of a hat in a way because what you do is – you have to do it – it has to happen from the first moment; or else, it doesn't, it's not something that you lay on people, it's something that you live. You come in there; I come in there in my own particular academic regalia, which is some kind of hat. If it's a Friday class I wear white because my *santo* is Orishala [A Yoruba divinity, the God of Whiteness, creator of humankind]. Orishala's day is Friday, and you wear white. 'Why are you wearing white? Wow? You kinda cool, Professor. What's going on?' And I launch.

> I launch into it. And I expect people – I set up the desks in a circle and do all those things we know to do to start a dialogical process. If it works, it works because from the beginning there may be three, four five people who get into that . . . And they [the students] get into it and I have paintings and pictures . . . as result of this, people are touched. Their core is touched. Because I'm sharing my core. I'm coming from my core. I'm coming from the things that matter most to me; I'm following my passion . . . and allowing myself to be touched; and allowing myself to be vulnerable as a model for what I, not 'expect' because you can't expect people to do that, . . . but there are others, who 'Wow . . . Oh, my goodness, Dr. S., this is such a different class. I am so glad I took it. I was so afraid that you were gonna do public speaking things.' I say, 'Yes, we'll do a little public speaking'. But the gist of the class is, 'Who are you? Where are you from? What are your dreams? How do you present your dreams in a format that includes body language, vocal training somewhat . . . ?' All those things which I have done in my life – acting, studying. That I feel are beneficent to a variety of people.

Doug's critical awareness of vulnerability that does not demand similar confessional behaviour from students stands out here. The delicate incorporation of acting and/in teaching is also noticeable here. When working with a student who presents a personal issue to Doug and who is having trouble staying on track with assignments, he drew on this acting training in his response:

> What I draw on: I draw on basics of acting, acting training. 'As if'. I dwell on my 'as if'. As if I were she, how do I respond her in kind. I have to be her. I have to inculcate that raw emotion, and that disappointment, and that anomie that she describes. . . . The 'as if' is something that Freire shares with [the theatre practitioner Sanford] Meisner or with [the Russian actor and theatre director Constantin] Stanislavski which is getting close to the people. . . . What I have to do is find an appropriate response which will energize her and get her back on track. At the same time, I have to acknowledge the pain, which I feel is real. Which I feel myself in my own career.

Reminiscence is woven into this as well as the opening excerpt of this sketch, as Doug reflects on the length and challenges of his own career. His openness about his praxis and the particular way he utilised his acting training stands out in the excerpts of this sketch, bringing to life the exquisite nuances of the way life experiences in other fields enrich classroom pedagogy.

Sketch 3: ideology (Freire meets for-profit)

Throughout all of these for-profit experiences, Doug's resilient identity as a Freirean provides a constant ontological grounding for him. Considering Pine, Doug lamented:

> I have one lady who has spent $135,000 so far and has not yet reached a dissertation stage . . . So there's a lot of scamming going on out there. . . . It's a sharkish sea to swim in. . . . As a teacher what you do is fall in love with your students, as a Freirean of course everything is *empapado de amor*, everything is soaked with love, so you fall in love. I've sent checks, I've bought computers. . . . Because people end up in [X] city with their roof caving in. . . .You cannot believe the stories but the stories are there and they're real.

His life trajectory emerged when he reflected on current events:

> I didn't think I will be in this position at my age. You know what I'm saying, like I don't wanna be a grumbling old codger. Saying, you know, (grumbles) 'I told you', I don't wanna do that. It's not me. It's not what I care about. What I care about is continuing to communicate my vision and my utopian feelings about the chance that we will all survive and flourish. And how the hell do we that? (laughing). . . . How do you keep on the path? Trudging the path when everything conspires against you?

Announcing – in the Freirean sense – that he does not want to be a 'grumbling old codger', Doug again engages again in (self) 'healing' humour around his age and gender in a poignant reflection on sustaining utopistics throughout the lifespan. This Freirean concept of 'utopistics' refers to

> the serious assessment of historical alternatives, the exercise of our judgment as to the substantive rationality of alternative possible historical systems. It is the sober, rational, and realistic evaluation of human social systems, the constraints on what they can be, and the zones open to human creativity. Not the face of the perfect

> (and inevitable) future, but the face of an alternative, better, and historically possible (but far from certain) future.
>
> (Wallerstein 1998 in Teodoro and Torres 2007, 1)

Doug recognised that the challenges of these settings necessitate a renegotiation of this ideological identity:

> All of the Freirean impulses that I have, naturally and through reading Paulo's theory and Paulo's experiences, are challenged in both cases – [in] one they're challenged by the fact that I don't get in front of the people corporally; I don't have that exchange of energy. In the other situation, because the kids come with all of their cybernetic 'accoutrements', and they're like this (illustrates student occupied by a gadget) or they've got their earphones in. So the first thing I have to do is get rid of all of that, in other words, let them put all of that aside, and just see me. And just understand that I'm there to share my experience, strength, and hope, my life trajectory, everything with them through the course and that I want them to respond in kind. So as Paulo knew, that's not simple to begin with. And it can't be 'blah, blah', what he called 'blah, blah', was, you know, just being nice or *chichia*. [There's] that book about no *chichia* so no 'blah blah', no *chichia*. So what's left? What's left is translating hard-core curriculum, you know, into dialogical format. This is something that almost nobody is doing these days. And almost nobody even understands why it would be important to do. So you're working against the current wherever you go.

The translation of what Doug calls the 'hard-core curriculum' as warranted by the for-profits, and the possibilities of agency by critical educators here, sharply stands out; I argue that Doug is articulating one of the largest gaps in the work on Freire in HE: in this 'belly of the beast', two epistemological currents collide in what Doug alludes to as an isolating pedagogical experience. While Doug, in this quote, is referring to Oak (the brick and mortar), I argue that this ideological schism could easily play out in distance education, in a virtual classroom for an instructor at Pine (the online). In considering his own pedagogical strategies in the face of this gap, he noted the challenges that Freire also had:

> When Freire was still the bearded professor, the Socratic, he couldn't understand nor get through to these people. His wife tapped him on the shoulder and said, 'Paulo, change your language, change

> your language, talk the language of the people that you're talking to, because they're wise'. Paulo knew that but he didn't know how to make the switch.

This excerpt brings up the humanity of Freire and the important recognition by his first wife, the educator Elza Freire, and her understanding of 'talking the language of the people'. The preverbal curtain of this sketch closes with Doug and me having a serious discussion for the need for continued work and translation of work on Elza, an illustration of the *inéditos viáveis* in our own work and the fluid nature of our own positionalities beyond this research as intergenerational colleagues.

Sketch 4: the future of these educational settings (a 'vanguard')

This final and forward-looking sketch is a short narrative embodying the Freirean concept of 'announcing' one's current situation and possible futures.

When discussing whether or not these for-profit spaces were perceived as 'deficit' spaces for students and faculty, Doug stressed the importance of 'making them work for students':

> See, there's a whole flip side of this. Which is [that] the [so-called] 'deficit' spaces are full of the students that – that would never be or go to a traditional university for a variety of reasons including choice. So we are dealing with what I look as a kind of crazy vanguard. And the vanguard is these are the children of immigrants. . . . My family was marvellous in some ways and very destructive in other ways. But at least they gave me a sense of myself because it allowed me, and in my father's case, pushing me toward getting the best education in America. Now that education is further away than ever from the majority of people. It's a joke. It is a myth. You know, the Ivy League. The Ivy League! What is the Ivy League? It's some kind of floating phenomenon and it doesn't really play into anybody's life. THESE are the universities. These 'non-acceptable' – these are the universities of the future. Believe you me. I don't feel like I am in some kind of limbo or underworld. I feel like I'm jumping into the middle of 21st Century when all universities will be like this.

The idea of these spaces and the participants in them as a *vanguard* does not present a panacea to the inequalities of these settings (presented in this paper's introduction), but it certainly presents a challenge to any dismissal of these settings *based on* these inequalities. This is particularly true for critical educators who may resist these spaces, and who may be, necessarily and importantly, building alternative educational spaces. Mutual-exclusivity is not necessary here – critical educators are needed across educational settings. Instead, it suggests the need for re-examining for-profit spaces by critical educators, particularly students' and faculty's agency to choose not to go to a 'traditional university'. Ideas of 'deficit', 'non-acceptable', and 'limbo or underworld' spaces are flipped on their head, instead seen, to draw on Doug's quote above, a 'vanguard', 'the universities of the future', and a mid-twenty-first-century institution.

Discussion and conclusion: nuanced possibilities for feminist pedagogies

Tracing Doug's autobiographical, pedagogical, and ideological experiences in the first three sketches and his understanding of the future of these spaces in the final sketch has been an explorative look at age, gender, ideological, and online identities. What each of the fields – masculinities and HE from critical and feminist perspectives, masculinities (and other identities) online, and masculinities and aging from a critical, feminist gerontological perspective – offers to research in teaching in HE emerges through these sketches.

The idea of a sketch gives the freedom to present an incomplete vignette as a potential starting point for what may be more polished into continuing professional development (CPD) 'reflection pieces' (see Burke and Crozier, 2013) for practitioners. Thinking of concrete possibilities of CPD in these spaces is critical because the patchwork and fluid nature of educational work in neoliberal settings requires an enormous amount of self-reflection that is not served by most existing for-profit CPD. This lack of critical CPD is implied in Doug's responses about the rudimentary, online content that he is expected to complete: what he describes as biannual 'loyalty tests'. Two aspects of this self-reflection are (1) how these teachers understand new institutional roles that are created as part of universities' (entrepreneurial) quests to distinguish themselves, such as Doug's role as a 'mentor–assessor' and (2) the particular emotional labour that these new institutional roles imply. How to reach for-profit administrators and engage with them about the need for this critical CPD is another related issue that deserves much more work.

I argue that these sketches open up space to consider the dialectics present in distance education, including around masculinities, ideologies, and age, and push us to consider how to engage with the discomfort that these complex social identifiers cause across these three subfields. Sketches, such as the ones emerging from this research, allow for space to play with concepts across the three fields recognising the incompleteness, inconclusion, and unaccomplishedness of the researcher's relationship to the fields. They allow for, to employ Freirean language, an 'ingenous' (common sense) curiosity about the relationship of these fields to transform into the methodologically rigorous 'epistemological curiosity' (Freire 1998). How does scholarship around masculinities online reinvigorate gender and education scholars' thinking around 'the possibility of understanding gender that is not constituted by masculinity' (Haywood & Mac an Ghaill 2012, 589) and vice versa? What is the importance of centring narratives of expert educators in these discussions from a critical feminist geronotological perspective? In this study's case, to adapt the earlier quote from Freixas, Luque, and Reina (2012, 56), the 'complex and subtle life' of older educators like Doug 'would appear to be a wide field, open to thinking and critical and reflective research, in which their voices and experience are revealed to be essential tools'. Doug's experience is a highly nuanced example of this freedom to 'choose a lifestyle' and 'manner of aging that [one] prefers' (56).

There are rich possibilities for feminist pedagogies to be cultivated within these spaces of distance education – these 'vangaurd spaces' – but these possibilities are highly nuanced, and thinking through these nuances demands theoretical and methodological creativity, which I have attempted to cultivate through the consideration of theoretical 'future directions' and methodological 'sketches'.

Ultimately, I argue that as Doug examines central liminalities in his work and recognises his own *inéditos viáveis* as an educator, we see a concrete manifestation of the future directions of the defined three subfields. To draw once more on Freire (1998):

> . . . And here we have arrived at the point from which perhaps we should have departed: the unfinishedness of our being. In fact, this unfinishedness is essential to our human condition. Whenever there is life, there is unfinishedness, though only among women and men it is possible to speak of awareness of unfinishedness.
>
> (52)

Embracing Doug's deep awareness of the unfinishedness of work in these less traditional spaces is the cause for action: if this is indeed twenty-first century educational work, there is much work to be done by critical educators in solidarity with these vanguard students and faculty.

Acknowledgements

My deep and sincere thanks to Doug for his engagement with me on this project; to Professor Penny Jane Burke, whose feedback has deeply influenced my thinking on this article; to the two anonymous reviewers for their time providing me with extremely constructive feedback; to Professor Anu Aneja, for her constant support of this submission; and to my colleague at the 2016 Comparative and International Education Society Post Foundational Approaches panel for the Alanis reference.

This work was supported by the 2014 Fundamental Research Funds for the Comprehensive Construction of the Discipline of Education, Faculty of Education, Beijing Normal University; the US–UK Fulbright Commission; and the Paulo Freire Institute-UK, Centre for Educational Research in Equalities, Policy and Pedagogy, Roehampton University.

References

Allen, I. E., and J. Seaman. 2013. "2012 – Changing Course: Ten Years of Tracking Online Education in the United States." Learning Consortium. Accessed July 1. http://onlinelearningconsortium.org/survey_report/changing-course-ten-years-tracking-online-education-united-states/

American Psychological Association. 2015. "Why Practitioners Need Information About Working with Older Adults." Accessed February 24. http://www.apa.org/pi/aging/resources/guides/practitioners-should-know.aspx.

Ball, Stephen J. 2012. *Global Education Inc.: New Policy Networks and the Neoliberal Imaginary*. New York: Routledge.

Biggs, S. 2008. "Aging in a Critical World: The Search for Generational Intelligence." *Journal of Aging Studies* 22 (2): 115–119. doi:10.1016/j.jaging.2007.12.016

Biggs, Simon, Irja Haapala, and Ariela Lowenstein. 2011. "Exploring Generational Intelligence as a Model for Examining the Process of Intergenerational Relationships." *Ageing and Society* 31 (7): 1107–1124.

Britzman, D. P. 1997. "The Tangles of Implication." *Qualitative Studies in Education* 10 (1): 31–7.

Brown, Abram. 2012. "School's Out for Bridgepoint Education: Shares Slammed after Accreditation Denial." Forbes.com. Accessed May 16, 2014.

Burke, Penny Jane. 2011. "Masculinity, Subjectivity and Neoliberalism in Men's Accounts of Migration and Higher Educational Participation." *Gender and Education* 23 (2): 81–100.

Burke, Penny Jane, and Gill Crozier. 2013. *Teaching Inclusively: Changing Pedagogical Spaces*. Higher Education Academy, London: Roehampton University. https://www.srhe.ac.uk/downloads/events/103_TeachingInclusively ResourcePack.pdf.

Burke, Penny Jane, Gill Crozier, Barbara Read, Julie Hall, Jo Peat, and Becky Francis. 2013. *Formations of Gender and Higher Education Pedagogies Final Report (GaP)*. York: Higher Education Academy (HEA).

Chase, Susan E. 2010. "Narrative Inquiry: Multiple Lenses, Approaches, Voices." In *Qualitative Educational Research: Readings in Reflexive Methodology and Transformative Practice*, edited by Wendy Luttrell, 208–236. New York: Routledge.

Clegg, Sue. 2008. "Femininities/Masculinities and a Sense Self – Thinking Gendered Academic Identities and the Intellectual Self." *Gender and Education* 20 (3): 209–221.

Freire, Paulo. 1998. *Pedagogy of Freedom: Ethics, Democracy, and Civic Courage, Critical Perspectives Series*. Lanham, MD: Rowman and Littlefield.

Freixas, Anna, Bárbara Luque, and Amalia Reina. 2012. "Critical Feminist Gerontology: In the Back Room of Research." *Journal of Women and Aging* 24 (1): 44–58.

Hansen, Alissa. 2015. "For-profit Schools vs. Non-profit Schools." Global Post, Last Modified May 16, 2014. Accessed February 26. http://everydaylife.globalpost.com/forprofit-schools-vs-nonprofit-schools-17880.html.

Haywood, Chris, and Máirtín Mac an Ghaill. 2012. "'What's Next for Masculinity?' Reflexive Directions for Theory and Research on Masculinity and Education." *Gender and Education* 24 (6): 577–592.

Hey, Valerie, and Carole Leathwood. 2009. "Passionate Attachments: Higher Education, Policy, Knowledge, Emotion and Social Justice." *Higher Education Policy* 22 (1): 101–118.

Hooks, Bell. 2010. *Teaching Critical Thinking: Practical Wisdom*. New York: Routledge.

Kendall, Lori. 2011. "Community and the Internet." *The Handbook of Internet studies* 11: 309–325.

Morissette, Alanis, and Guy Sigsworth. 2008. "Incomplete [recorded by Alanis Morissette]." In *On Flavors of Entanglement [CD]*. Santa Monica, CA: Universal Music.

Romão, J. E. 2007. "Chapter 9: Sociology of Education or the Education of Sociology? Paulo Freire and the Sociology of Education." In *Critique and Utopia: New Developments in the Sociology of Education in the Twenty-first Century*, edited by Carlos Alberto Torres and António Teodoro, viii, 184. Lanham, MD: Rowman and Littlefield.

Sanchez, C. 2014. Part-Time Professors Demand Higher Pay; Will Colleges Listen? All Things Considered: National Public Radio (NPR) (News). http://www.npr.org/templates/transcript/transcript.php?storyId=268427156

Starcher, Keith. 2014. "Tomorrow's Professor Msg. #1377 TP Special Announcement – Understanding Part-time Online Instructors." Stanford

Center for Teaching and Learning. Accessed January 15. https://tomprof.stanford.edu/posting/1377-0

Teodoro, António, and Carlos Alberto Torres. 2007. "Introduction: Critique and Utopia in the Sociology of Education." In *Critique and Utopia: New Developments in the Sociology of Education in the Twenty-first Century*, edited by Carlos Alberto Torres and António Teodoro, 1–10. Lanham, MD: Rowman and Littlefield.

Torres, Carlos Alberto. 2007. "Paulo Freire, Education, and Transformative Social Justice Learning." In *Critique and Utopia: New Developments in the Sociology of Education in the Twenty-first Century*, edited by Carlos Alberto Torres and António Teodoro, 155–160. Lanham, MD: Rowman and Littlefield.

US Department of Education, National Center for Education Statistics. 2013. "Digest of Education Statistics." http://nces.ed.gov/fastfacts/display.asp?id=74.

Webster, Jeffrey Dean, Ernst T. Bohlmeijer, and Gerben J. Westerhof. 2010. "Mapping the Future of Reminiscence: A Conceptual Guide for Research and Practice." *Research on Aging* 32 (4): 527–564.

4 Feminist pedagogy and social media

A study on their integration and effectiveness in training budding women entrepreneurs

Mangala Vadivu Vivakaran and Neelamalar Maraimalai

Introduction

Gender gap is the primary outcome of the social inequalities faced by a particular individual or group based on their gender. Gender gap denotes the dissimilarities that individuals face in their social, political, intellectual, cultural or economic attainments owing to their gender. Discriminations based on gender will manifest themselves in all areas of development. In India, the obvious presence of gender inequalities can be seen in various sectors such as health, education, economy and public life. Indian women face discrimination at a very early stage; the child mortality rate is higher for girls than for boys (Census India 2011). When viewed through the educational spectrum, gender disparity in rural areas is relatively high, and overall, almost 41% of women claimed that they have never experienced a basic school-level education (Census India 2011). Alesina and Barro (2001) have observed that literacy and schooling are the two crucial factors for economic growth. The enormous level of gender inequalities present in the educational sector is primarily due to the confinement and restriction of women to their socially constructed images (handling gendered roles and responsibilities). In professional life, men and women with the same work experience tend to receive unequal payment (Waris and Viraktamath 2013). Attainment in the entrepreneurial and the business sphere also remains to be very low due to inadequate training and knowledge possessed by Indian women in this sector.

Entrepreneurship is one province where the role of women is growing and gaining importance exponentially. Women entrepreneurs form an unexploited power source that can be utilised for escalating the development rate of a nation (Minniti and Naudé 2010). They are viewed to be the chief catalyst of any economic advancement. Brush (2012) describes the rise of women entrepreneurship as a 'New Women's Movement'.

Despite these glorified perspectives on women entrepreneurship, there is the existence of a wide gender gap that has been identified and studied by many researchers in this area (Kaushal, Negi, and Singhal 2014; Sarfaraz, Faghih, and AsadiMajd 2014; Tambunan 2009; Wilson, Kickul, and Marlino 2007). In the field of entrepreneurship, gender gap denotes the difference in the number of people involved in entrepreneurial activities – motives to start a business, business growth and performance – in terms of gender.

The Global Entrepreneurship Monitor (Anon 2012) claimed that there are more than 187 million women engaged in entrepreneurship across the world, but in India, successful women entrepreneurs are rare to be found. The proportion of women entrepreneurs worldwide has escalated from 35% in 2004 to 41% in 2011. These developments exclude the existing scenario in Brazil and in India where a declining trend was recorded (Waris and Viraktamath 2013). Other than a few exceptional businesswomen, entrepreneurs are observed to fall in the informal sector of the economy (Minniti 2009). The informal sector constitutes women (lacking in education and training) who take up entrepreneurship purely for their survival needs – necessity entrepreneurs.

Due to the patriarchal roots of the Indian societal set-up, entrepreneurship is conventionally placed in the male domain. As a result of this, Indian women are observed to face many denigrations and barriers in their entrepreneurial journey in the past as well as in the present (Vijay Anand and Panchanatham 2011).

Indian women entrepreneurs form an adversely excluded group, as they represent only 10% of the total entrepreneurs present in India, yielding a gross output of only 3.5% in the small-scale industrial sector (Kaushal, Negi, and Singhal 2014). Women not only rank low in starting and running their business, but they also face many challenges in establishing a sustainable enterprise. According to Kaushal, Negi, and Singhal (2014), the exit rate of new businesses is generally high (40–50%), but the exit rate of firms owned by women is recorded to be even higher. These statistical facts clearly portray the belittled status of women entrepreneurs in India. Irrespective of the various governmental initiatives and resources provided, women entrepreneurs seem to manage fewer businesses, gain lesser money and show dawdling growth when compared to their male counterparts.

Literature review

'Gender' denotes the set of beliefs or characteristics that are held to be appropriate for the members belonging to one sex rather than the other (Archer and Lloyd 2002; Lippa 2005). The term is independent of a person's biological sex and is dependent on the social construction of a particular sex. Children's exposure to gender socialisation (at an early age) aids them in gaining knowledge concerning gender stereotypes and gender roles. Gender socialisation (occurring via parents, schools, peers and media) encourages children to limit themselves to their gendered roles (Kite, Deaux, and Haines 2008). These factors continue to influence the attitude and behaviour of the children through their adulthood. Hence, they tend to possess gendered assumptions regarding the different roles expected from men and women, including entrepreneurial functions (Marlow and Patton 2005).

Gender and entrepreneurship

Women's entrepreneurship previously served as an 'invisible field' of study, as it has been ignored by many scholars historically (Hamilton 2013). Though research on women entrepreneurship has increased in the recent years (Brush et al. 2006), women still tend to believe that entrepreneurship is a less favourable career option for them in comparison to men (Langowitz and Minniti 2007). The conventional gender-belief system holding a hierarchical angle where feminine traits are valued less compared to masculine traits (Crannie-Francies et al. 2003) may be one of the prime reasons for this particular scenario. Entrepreneurship continues to be associated with masculine attributes due to gendered societal values and roles making women an excluded group. These stereotypes result in the less normative and undesirable conditions provided by the society for women to enter an entrepreneurial career (Baughn, Chua, and Neupert 2006). Many scholars point out that entrepreneurship itself is a gendered process (Ahl 2002; Delmar and Holmquist 2004; Winn 2005). For instance, Marlow's subordination system of gender and sex prioritises men to be the primary factor for understanding women's entrepreneurial experience (Marlow 2002).

Ajzen's theory (1991) of planned behaviour (that proposes that personal attraction, subjective norms and perceived behavioural control are the three antecedents that shape individual behaviour intentions) is the most used theory by entrepreneurship scholars to investigate the entrepreneurial intentions among individuals. Many such studies

(Liñan and Chen 2009; Liñan, Roomi, and Santos 2010; Moriano et al. 2011) have yielded a similar result where men exhibited a higher intention of setting up an enterprise in comparison to women.

Family support plays a crucial role in shaping the entrepreneurial career of any individual (Jennings and McDougald 2007). However, in the case of women, work–family conflict (gendered roles and responsibilities) is observed to affect their entrepreneurial journey, as they tend to have greater responsibilities than men inside the house (Eddleston and Powell 2012; Lippa 2005). These roles and responsibilities constitute an unavoidable weakness for the women entrepreneurs while competing with their male counterparts (Ahl 2006).

In addition, the foremost challenges faced by women in implementing their business ideas and developing a successful enterprise include the lack of adequate training, knowledge and access to information concerning entrepreneurship. Especially in India, women are perceived to have less exposure to higher education and training facilities for enhancing their entrepreneurial skills (Bertaux and Crable 2007). These factors, combined with the absence of career guidance, make them inaccessible to the various business support services offered by the government as well as private organisations. Various other factors such as limited mobility, work–family interface, women's safety, lack of societal and financial support seem to increase the challenges that women entrepreneurs have to overcome before succeeding in their venture. These obstructions result in jeopardising the development and existence of sustainable women entrepreneurs in India and other developing countries.

Feminist pedagogy

In order to educate and train Indian women for their entrepreneurial journey, an effective learning platform that caters to their needs and flexibility is an indispensable requirement. The conventional lecture-based learning system will not serve as an efficient solution for this purpose, as it does not focus entirely on the needs of the learners. It is essential to adopt a learner-centric educational model for bringing out the voices of the learners which can aid in transforming socially oppressed Indian women into confident and independent entrepreneurs.

Feminist pedagogy which falls under the critical learning theories is claimed to be an effective tool for creating an empowering learning environment (Hayes and Flannery 2000). Schweitzer (2001) stated that there exist a wide array of definitions explaining the concept of feminist pedagogy. The fundamental notion of feminist pedagogy is the process of restructuring the classroom into a learning community that encourages collaborative and participatory actions among the learners corresponding to the developmental needs of both women and men. A feminist classroom serves as a liberatory environment where the students learn to respect each other's differences. It aims at creating a learning atmosphere where the students can voice out and share their skills, opinions and talents within the learning community. Feminist pedagogy is a student-centric learning theory that views knowledge construction as a democratic process (Crabtree 2009). A few common and essential factors of a feminist learning system include collaboration, interaction, connection and empowerment (Kirkup 2005; Nawratil 1999; Tisdell 2000). Feminist pedagogy relies on building a safe and diverse learning community where the teacher and students can share and collaborate on the knowledge construction process and the learning progression of all, within the community (Chinn 2001).

According to Kimmel (1999), an online democratic classroom depicts a learning community in which equality in power and flexibility in teacher–student roles prevails. Feminist pedagogy, adopting a similar democratic approach of learning, aims towards the decentralisation of power and authority within the learning environment (Stanley-Spaeth 2000). In order to experience a successful feminist classroom, it is crucial for the lecture to build an environment ensuring that every learner has a voice (Crabtree 2009). Hence, a feminist teacher is equivalent to a 'moderator' or a 'facilitator', who ensures that the community collaborates effectively by directing the learners towards achieving the maximum understanding (Forsythe 2003).

Many studies have been conducted by incorporating feminist pedagogy and analysing its effectiveness for andragogy in the past (Lawrence 1997; Ryan 2001; Sandlin 2005; Tisdell 2000). According to Maher and Tetreault (2008), feminism enhances the classic mode of andragogy by challenging hierarchy and authority and by overcoming gender inequality issues within the learning environment. Two recent studies on feminism in adult education are discussed here. Carney et al. (2012) had experimented feminist pedagogy in a small, private university in the United States. They merged feminist learning with a course on women's rights named 'Resistance & Rights: Global Women'. By assessing the performance of the students, they were able to identify that feminist pedagogy benefits both the faculty and students equally. The faculties were benefited, as they were able to discuss the course strategies and class dynamics with the students in addition to the actual course content which aided them in performing a formative evaluation of the course for tailoring the course content and structure based on the learners' needs. Students were also able to gain a thorough understanding by expressing their personal experiences and relating it with the content learnt and by collaborating with their peers without any obstructions due to the presence of the decentralised nature of power within the learning community. In the second study, Lamont (2014) explored feminist pedagogy by integrating it into a module named 'Interpersonal Skills for Nurses' for students attending B.Sc. (Hons) Nursing programme. The feminist class was structured including various techniques – communication exercises to enhance interactivity within the classroom, knowledge exchange sessions, practical role-play learning sessions, and so on – to provide an inclusive and valuable feminist learning experience. The feedback that was collected at the end of the semester highlighted that the students found the new pedagogical style to be fascinating due to their active role within the classroom. It also aided them in enhancing their personal development and identity as a nurse.

Overall, feminist goals such as 'atmosphere of mutual respect, shared leadership, action-oriented field work, trust and community' (Hezekiah 1993, 54) are observed to yield an enhanced learning environment (Nelsen 1981; Schniedewind 1985; Torney-Purta 1983), making it suitable for entrepreneurial training.

The social web and Web 2.0 tools

The growth of technology has been exponential with the advent of Web 2.0. Web 2.0 is a term used to distinguish its precursor Web 1.0, a name given to the initial phase of World Wide Web's revolution. Web 2.0 refers to the advancements in the aesthetic elements such as the participatory, interactive and more collaborative culture of the web, in addition to the technical upgradation of the same (O' Reilly 2005).

The tools present in Web 2.0 synonymously known as social media tools are currently influencing a major change to the conventional pedagogical system. It increases the awareness and effectiveness of student-centric learning environments where the students become more participatory, collaborative and act as 'active learners'. Active as opposed to passive learners are better at understanding complex information and transfer the concepts learnt in one setting to another and are more likely to retain information (Bransford, Brown, and Cocking 1999). According to Rovai (2007), educators should encourage active learning where the focus is on motivating and finding ways to lead the students to the discovery or the creation of knowledge rather than the transfer of knowledge from teacher to student.

Web 2.0 focuses mainly on the relationships and interactions within its users rather than the content present in it. It highlighted a major paradigm shift of the web users from being passive participants whose role was limited to viewing the web content to active co-participants who have become the creators of the web content (Baird and Fisher 2009). The advanced web integrates various social features such as social softwares (social networking sites), blogging, folksonomies, discussion forum, wikis and video sharing sites and it emphasises more on user-generated content and collaboration.

Integration of Web 2.0 and feminist pedagogy

It is apparent that the feminist pedagogy correlates well with the concept of Web 2.0, as the ultimate aim of both is to enhance participation, interactions and collaboration among its users for the greater good of escalating the users' knowledge and understanding. Hence, an appropriate use of the social and instructional technology can aid in building a virtual feminist environment for active learning.

Beyond technological advancements, computer-mediated communication can be utilised to create a pedagogical framework that encourages active learning through 'constant collaborative conservation' (Elliott and Woloshyn 1997). Critical engagement with the online social platform has been perceived to generate a collaborative learning environment that supports the basic goals of feminism and feminist pedagogy (Ewell 2000; Schweitzer 2001). Kirkup (2005) asserts that the online feminist classroom emphasises the importance of students' voices, connections formed, cooperation and negotiation within the learning community. Here, learning is observed to occur through socially interactive conversations and non-threatening intensive collaboration (Lai and Lu 2009). Many researchers (Lai and Lu 2007; Palloff and Pratt 2005; Torrens 2007; Turpin 2007) have supported the high educational potential of asynchronous online discussion boards (of the social web) due to various built-in factors including time–space flexibility, multi-linear and multiple modes of technologically enhanced discussion threads that can assist in the contribution of a deep and an enhanced learning process. Feminist asynchronous online discussions are claimed to enable the learners to transform themselves into knowledge developers rather than a passive consumer of knowledge (Lai and Lu 2009). Chick and Hassel (2009) contend that the incorporation of feminist learning techniques with the social web is vital for the learners of the present generation. The upcoming feminist derivations of virtual learning systems such as the Distributed Open Collaborative Courses depict the crucial role that feminist pedagogy is foreseen to play in future online learning systems (Balsamo et al. 2013).

Web 2.0 tools are built with the leverage of extreme access and mobility in order to service its users constantly, bridging the gap between feminist educators and learners who are geographically dispersed, resulting in the creation of new opportunities for feminist networking (Patterson 2012). Kramarae (2001) had identified that women from patriarchal societies with gendered responsibilities (homemaker, mother, wife, etc.) generally decide to opt for online courses, as they believe that online learning is the only option available to pursue their higher education. Also, women have also been found to gain a greater sense of deep learning and satisfaction in a virtual (asynchronous) discussion-based learning environments (Anderson and Haddad 2005; Caspi, Chajut, and Saporta 2008). Hence, it is vital to integrate feminist pedagogy with social media tools in order to build an ideal platform encompassing all the essential features that are required to reach and educate the emerging women entrepreneurs in India. Budding entrepreneurs must learn to develop the confidence and power to voice out their thoughts and opinion to empower themselves in order to initiate their entrepreneurial journey and to lead a successful business venture. Engaging them with an online and socially interactive feminist learning environment will assist in enabling them to overcome socially induced attributes such as shyness and reluctance. It will also aid in boosting their confidence level and to be more participatory in educating themselves along with others present inside the learning community. Another crucial purpose for employing feminist pedagogy for providing entrepreneurial training is that feminist learning is theorised to cultivate key roles exhibited by successful entrepreneurs including confident thinkers, determined creators, flexible collaborators and ambitious enquirers (Glasper, McEwing, and Richardson 2009).

Methodology

Experimental research design was employed in the study for analysing the effectiveness of utilising social media platform as a pedagogical tool for knowledge enhancement of emerging Indian women entrepreneurs. The pre-test for the experimental group was done by including various self-assessment questions regarding entrepreneurial knowledge in the registration form and the post-test was done by following the same technique in the feedback form which was provided at the end of the treatment (virtual workshop) (Table 4.1).

Table 4.1 Schematic representation of the experimental study.

Experimental group	*Registered Indian women entrepreneurs*
Pre-test	Assessing the entrepreneurial knowledge level using Registration form
Treatment	Social media learning – virtual workshop
Post-test	Assessing the entrepreneurial knowledge level after the workshop using feedback form

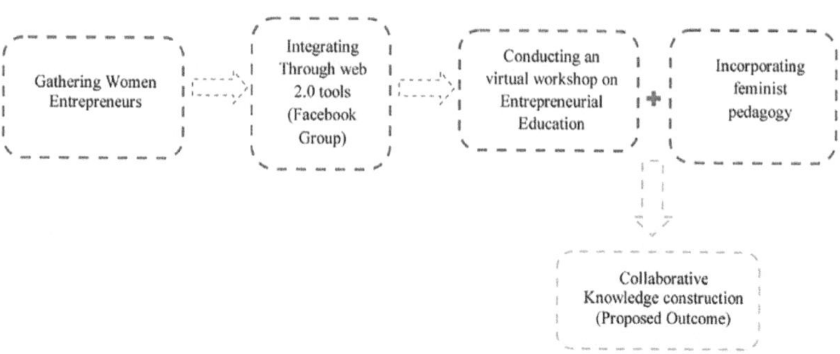

Figure 4.1 The research design used for the present study.

The research design for the present study can be divided into five phases as shown in Figure 4.1. In the initial phase, the researchers were involved in identifying and gathering potential learners who would be interested in attending an online workshop on entrepreneurial development. Open call for registrations were posted on multiple social media platforms and online groups focusing on women entrepreneurship in India. Interested people were requested to register themselves by filling an online registration form. The registration form contained basic demographic questions and a few question related to entrepreneurship for the purpose of assessing the knowledge of the participants before attending the workshop. According to Hayes and Flannery (2000), a large number of learners might disrupt a feminist class because the high enrolment rate forms a barrier in hearing out everyone's voice within the learning environment and for creating an effective learning community. The instructor might face challenges while monitoring and encouraging the active role of all the individuals present within the learning community and the learners might also find it difficult or take a longer duration to integrate among themselves in order to form a trustable learning community. Hence, for the present study, the registrations were kept limited and were closed once the registration count reached twenty. Of the 20 registered, 15 participants were filtered for the study based on the authenticity of the information provided by them during the registration phase. The filtered 15 participants were invited to join the official Facebook group of the workshop – Online Workshop for Professional Entrepreneurial Training for Women (OWPETW) before the day of the workshop. The participants were from diverse demographic backgrounds and were from various geographical locations dispersed across India. Almost 82% of the participants constituted married Indian women. Women falling under the age group of 25–35 years held the highest enrolment rate (73%) in the workshop. Women who were above 45 years of age had the least enrolment rate (4%). Though all the participants were educated, almost 60% of the women registered did not hold a proper full-time job position. They were mostly homemakers and women who were working from home or in part-time jobs.

The workshop was conducted for two days with a total of eight sessions. Periodic breaks were given between sessions for the participants' refreshments and relaxation. Table 4.2 showing the session schedule of the two-day workshop is provided here.

According to Webb, Allen, and Walker (2002), the six core principles of feminist pedagogy include the reformation of the relationship between teacher and student; empowerment; building community; privileging the individual voice; respect for diversity of personal experience and challenging traditional values. Each session of the

Table 4.2 Session schedule of the workshop.

S. No	*Agenda*
1	Introduction to entrepreneurship (definition and process)
2	Idea generation methods
3	Forms of business ownership. entrepreneurial terms and concepts – MVP, unique selling point, venture capitalist, angel investors, break even analysis
4	Structure of business plan
5	Marketing techniques with special reference to online marketing
6	Legal framework to start a business in India generation of financial assistance
7	Problems faced by Indian women entrepreneurs – A discussion within the participants
8	Feedback and discussion session

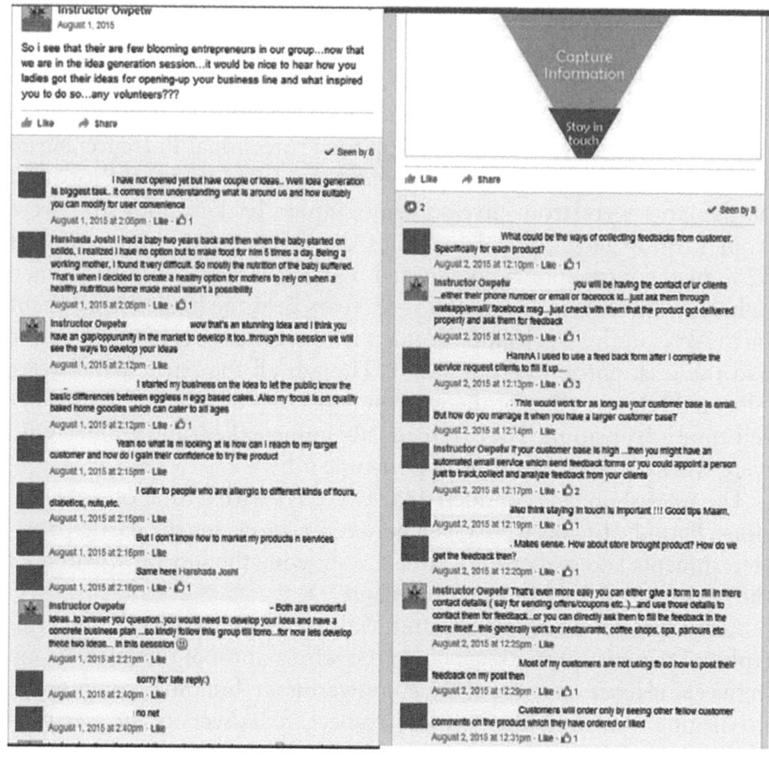

Figure 4.2 Screenshots of the virtual workshop conducted for the study.

workshop was designed to incorporate these principles by employing various techniques such as networking sessions, solving real-life problems, collaborative brainstorming, mapping idealisations and sharing relevant personal experiences. The participants were able to interact with each other and with the instructor in order to achieve a collaborative knowledge creation process within the learning community (Figure 4.2).

Analysis

Both qualitative and quantitative methods were employed for analysing the experimental study. McMullan and Vesgner (2001) state that ideally, satisfaction, learning and behavioural measures of the participants can be used for evaluating the effectiveness of any training programme. Data collected through the registration and feedback form of the participants were used to analyse the knowledge enhancement level of the learners. Content analysis of all the interactions within the learning community was adopted for assessing the learning and behavioural measures qualitatively. Social network analysis (SNA) was utilised to examine the behavioural measures of the participants. Moreover, the participants' comments (feedback) were used to analyse the satisfaction level of the workshop.

Content analysis

Content analysis for the study was done by extracting and coding the online discussions or interactions that occurred during the two-day workshop. A total of 258 comments were identified and coded. The researcher used the coding framework proposed by Garrison, Anderson, and Archer (2001) which viewed critical thinking as a four-stage process – triggering, exploration, integration and resolution. Feminist learning cascades under the critical pedagogy classification, making Garrison's framework an effective tool for evaluating the same. According to Garrison's model, the act of posting questions/issue/problem denotes the initial phase of a critical enquiry (triggering event). The explorative phase is one where the participants search for information relevant to the question posted and provides reflective comment/opinions regarding the problem. The third phase known as the integration phase is where the participants post the potential solution to the proposed problem by constructing meaning and developing ideas from the explorative phase. The final resolution phase is where the learning community evaluates and assesses the proposed solution in terms of feasibility and application.

It can be inferred from the above chart (Figure 4.3) that both triggering and integration post forms an equal share (approximately) of the overall discussion by occupying 24% and 25% in the discussion chart, respectively. Integration posts form the major part of the discussion sphere by covering 38% of the sphere. Resolution posts constitute the least proportion of sphere by occupying only 13% of the chart.

From the above inference, we can see that almost 24% of the comments acted as the triggering agents that had initiated various discussions during the workshop. It also denotes that with a relatively small learning community, the learners are able to voice out their queries openly without any communication barrier. Next to triggering, exploration posts were viewed as equally popular. Exploration can be justified as a common trait in online discussions where the core concept is

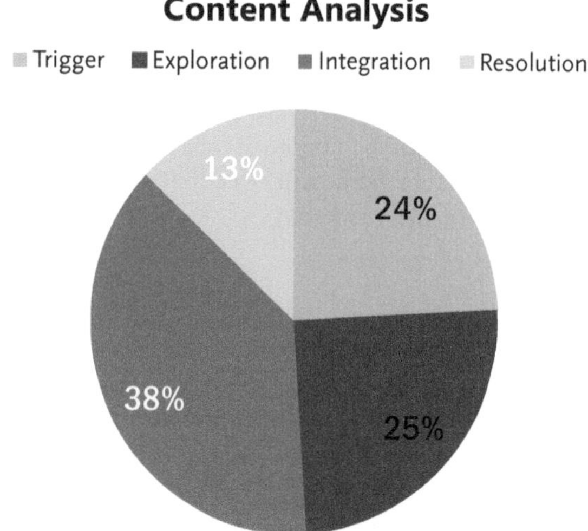

Figure 4.3 The pie chart representing the content analysis of the online discussions.

to share and compare information collectively for a better understanding of the problem involved. It is also crucial to note the high intensity of integration posts within the group, which denotes that the learners had moved beyond collaborating or comparing information. Additionally, they were able to construct ideas and propose many potential solutions regarding the issue/problem discussed. For instance, the workshop had a session on 'idea generation' in which concepts such as brainstorming and mind maps were discussed. After the sessions, the participants actively started to generate their own ideas and visualised them through mind maps. They also collaborated with their peers in order to mutually enhance each other's business ideas.

Quantitative analysis

Quantitative analysis was done by utilising the data collected from the participants through the registration and feedback forms, which were provided before and after the workshop, respectively. The awareness and knowledge level of a few basic entrepreneurial concepts of the participants before and after participating in the workshop are visualised in Figure 4.4. The concept of 'Minimum viable product' (MVP)

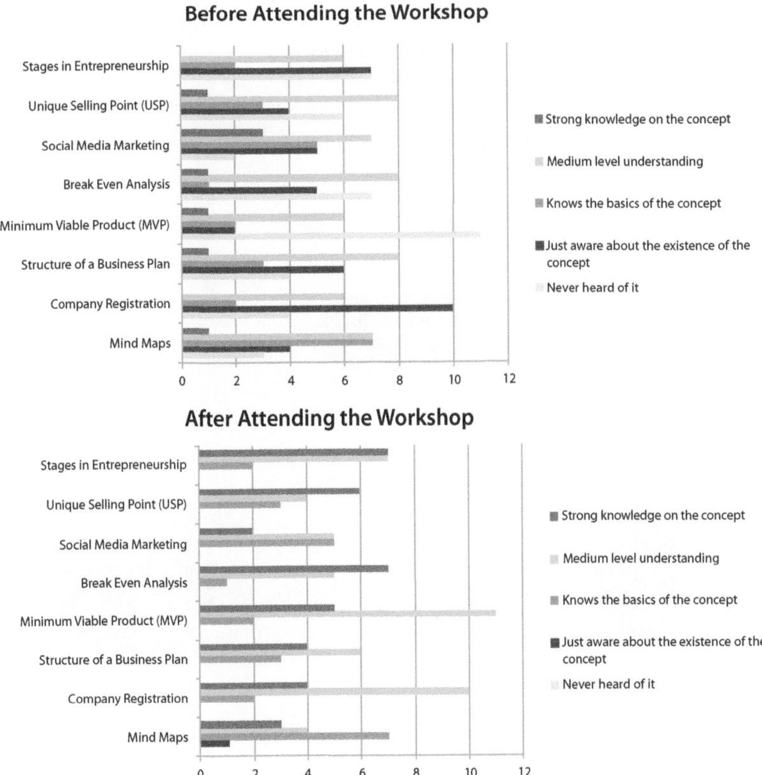

Figure 4.4 Knowledge assessment of the participants before and after attending the workshop.

was viewed to have the highest level (59%) of unawareness among the participants before conducting the workshop. It is apparent from the second bar chart (Figure 4.4) that the awareness level of the same was amplified and almost 54% of the participants had a strong knowledge on MVP. Information regarding company registration stands next to MVP in terms of unawareness (46%). By the end of the workshop, the knowledge level of the participants regarding company registration has escalated to 64%. Participants also appeared to enhance their knowledge on other basic entrepreneurial concepts discussed during the workshop.

Figure 4.5 shows the agreement level of registered participants regarding the various factors influencing women entrepreneurship in

Formal Training is necessary for entering the business world

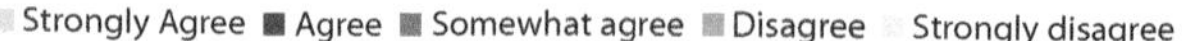

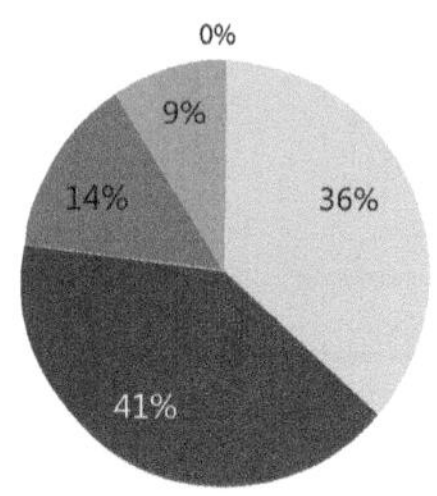

Proper training can reduce the risk involved and enhance your business

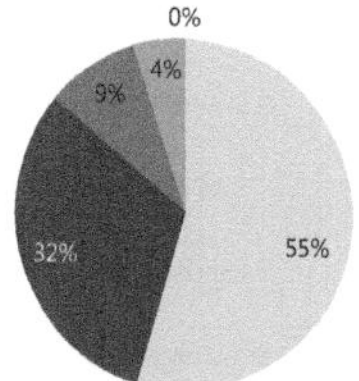

Women have less access to formal education/trair required for entrepreneurship

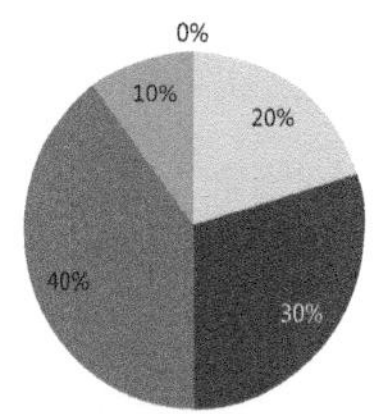

Women face more problems than men in the field of business

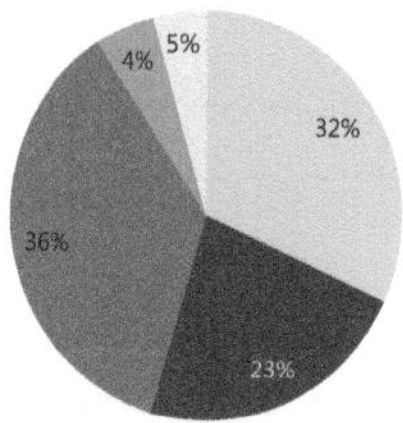

Inequality in gender previals in entrepreneurship

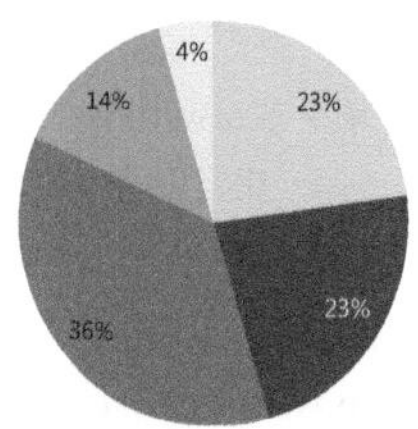

Figure 4.5 The pie charts representing the agreement level of the participants regarding various factors influencing women entrepreneurship in India.

India. It can be inferred from the graph that, of the 20 registered participants, 36% of them strongly agreed that formal training is mandatory before entering the entrepreneurial market and 87% of the participants felt that training is an essential requirement for the enhancement of any business/enterprise. Almost 90% of the participants claimed

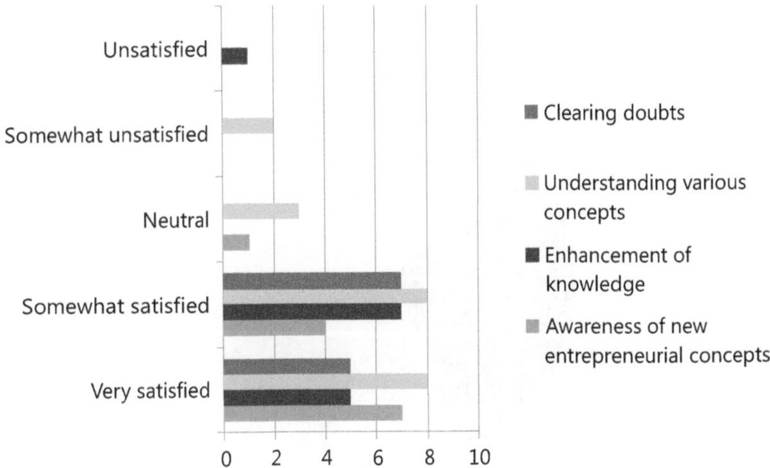

Figure 4.6 Satisfaction level of the participants.

that women have relatively less access to formal education or training to develop their entrepreneurial skills. Other than a few participants, most of them expressed that women tend to face more problems and experience gender inequality in the entrepreneurial market.

Figure 4.6 indicates the satisfaction level of the participants after attending the two-day workshop. It can be inferred from the bar graph that a large percentage of the participants were very much satisfied with the workshop regarding awareness of new entrepreneurial concepts (54%), enhancement of their knowledge (38%), understanding (38%) and clearing their doubts (42%). Only 8% of the participants conveyed that they were unsatisfied in terms of knowledge enhancement.

The pie chart (Figure 4.7) shows that 57% of the participants strongly agreed that the workshop assisted them to gain confidence and to develop their business to a next level. The bar graph (Figure 4.8) depicts the participants' preferences when they were asked to compare the traditional lecture-based workshops and the online discussion-based workshop concerning elements such as the level of understanding, interactivity and expressiveness of the participants present in both. It is apparent that the participants preferred the online discussion-based workshop over the conventional one in all the three elements of comparisons. Interactivity, flexibility in time and unlimited access to the course content were the three factors that were highlighted by the participants for preferring the online workshop. The workshop

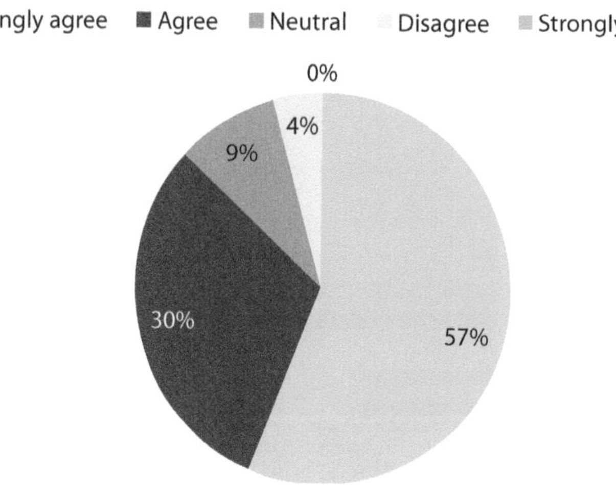

Figure 4.7 Participants' confidence boost after attending the workshop.

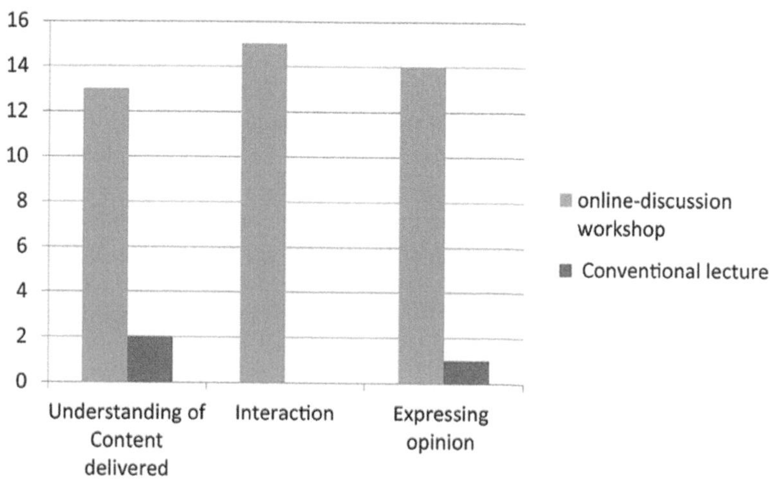

Figure 4.8 Participants' preference over online and conventional workshop.

adhered to the principles of feminist pedagogy in creating a safe and empowering environment, which aided the participants to voice out their doubts and opinions with confidence, thereby increasing interactivity. Similarly, the participants experienced a high level of time flexibility, as no strict time slots were followed and they had the freedom to engage with the course content 24×7. The participants were also able to refer to the content that was posted in previous sessions of the workshop with unlimited access to clarify their doubts or for recall purposes.

Social network analysis

SNA for digital networking platforms like Facebook is done by mining, extracting and analysing the network data obtained from the social networking sites. The data collection for the present study was done by using 'Netvizz' – a data mining application that is used by many researchers to extract and export Facebook network data in various standard file formats for analysis. The Network data of the OWPETW (2015) Facebook group were extracted for a time period of two days – the two days of the workshop.

From the extracted data, the overall engagement level of each post was calculated. The overall engagement denotes the sum of any engagement a particular post receives – likes, comments or shares.

The graphical representation of the calculated engagement of all the posts that were posted during the workshop can be viewed in Figure 4.9. The average engagement received by all the posts was calculated to be 5.79, which is relatively high. The average engagement shows that all the posts were engaged by the learning community on an average of more than five times during the workshop period. The yellow (Y) peak denotes the post that was posted and discussed during the idea-generating methods session on the first day of the workshop

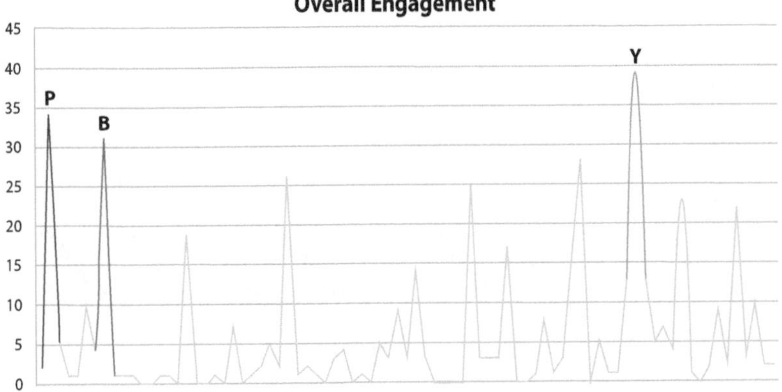

Figure 4.9 Engagement level of all the posts generated in the workshop.

which received the highest number of engagements. The pink peak (P) denotes the second highest post in terms of engagement; the post was regarding a discussion on problems faced by the Indian women entrepreneurs in establishing and surviving in the market. In this particular session, the participants were able to open up and express their personal experiences on the problems they had faced or were currently facing owing to their gender in the entrepreneurial spectrum. The presence and growth of a stable and trustable learning community assisted the participants to feel secure in posting various personal struggles faced by them in their day-to-day lives. Lack of independence, weak family and financial support, family commitments, limited access or mobility and so on constitute the major problems that were highlighted during the discussion. The mutual support system from the peers aided the participants in receiving suggestions and encouragements to overcome the issues being discussed. The blue peak (B) implies the post on marketing techniques (the first session of the second day) which ranks third in terms of engagement value. It is important to note that the discussions regarding the legal registration of an enterprise in India, creating a business plan and financial assistance were the few areas that acquired the least value on the engagement scale.

Figure 4.10 shows the engagement rate in a session-wise break down of the workshop. This graph supports the above inferences and clearly

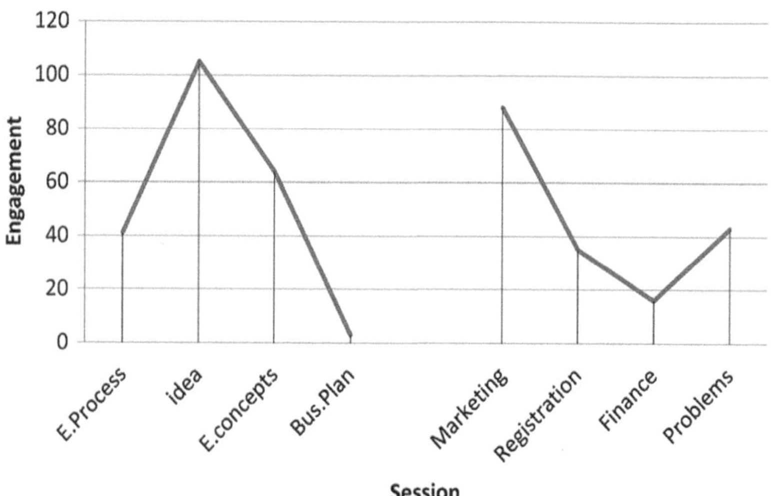

Figure 4.10 Engagement level of session-wise posts generated in the workshop.

depicts that the 'idea generation session' held on the first day of the workshop had the maximum engagement rate and the 'business plan session' had the least engagement rate. In the second day of the workshop, the marketing session tops the list in terms of engagement and the finance session stays at the bottom.

The network data of the OWPETW (2015) Facebook group that were mined and extracted from the Facebook network were fed into 'Gephi' – open source network visualisation software for analysing its network structure. Figure 4.11 is the output generated by the

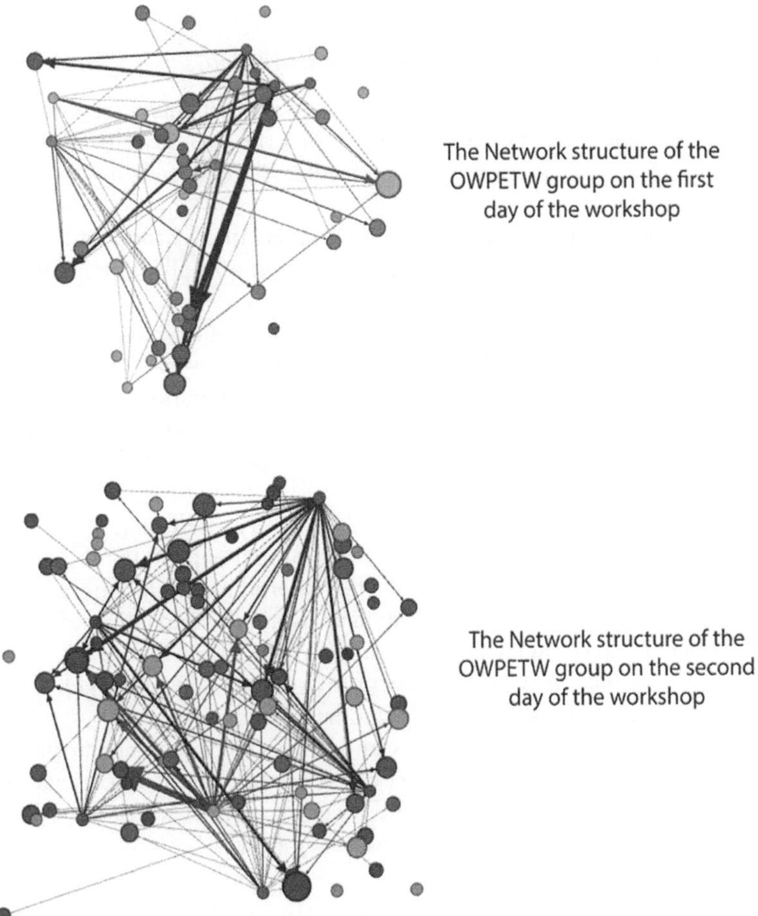

The Network structure of the OWPETW group on the first day of the workshop
The Network structure of the OWPETW group on the second day of the workshop

Figure 4.11 Network structure visualisation of the two-day virtual workshop.

visualisation software when the network data of first and second of the workshop were given as the inputs. The circles signify the 'post' that was posted in the group on that particular day of the workshop, whereas the lines and the arrows symbolise the interactions of the participants with that particular post. The size of the circle correlates with the engagement rate of a particular post-bigger circle signifies higher engagement and vice versa. By comparing the two network structures, it can be inferred that the first day of the workshop had a relatively low interaction and collaboration degree among the participants when compared with the second day's network structures.

Feedback and comments regarding the workshop

On the final session of the workshop, the participants were asked to give their opinions and feedback regarding the two-day virtual workshop. A few of their comments and feedback are listed below.

> I also need discussions and content on email. I learnt a lot . . . and Want to apply it all! All the best to you and all participants !!! Thank you very much
>
> Dear All and Ma'am, I totally enjoyed the two day Workshop and gained a lot of knowledge. Also the fellow participants were helpful. I would like to be a part of more such workshops in future.
>
> I was actually searching for the knowledge about entrepreneurship and entrepreneurs. This workshop helped me to get in-depth knowledge in the topics.
>
> Thank you [instructor name]. It was very interesting. Thanks to you I now want to make a video for my start-up. So thank you for that idea. Will go through all the material and will definitely get back to you in case if need any help especially in relation to social media marketing. Thank you and do keep in touch.
>
> It would be nice if interaction by voice (skype/google hangout . . .) can also be included in the future workshop
>
> Good response to queries and fairly good content, most was new for me. Awaiting the email with course content and discussion of interactive sessions. I found it very good! Most helpful, I need to put so many procedures into action now!

The feedback received was mostly optimistic in nature. From the above comments, we can infer that the participants were quite satisfied with the workshop. They were observed to value the discussions feed of the workshop (as many requested for the entire discussions feed – created during the workshop – to be compiled and emailed for future reference). It can also be noted that the participants appreciated the other participants for their help and inputs during the course of the workshop, hinting on the collaborative feminist learning structure followed during the workshop. One key suggestion that was given by a few participants was to include a video chat/voice calling session for the future programmes, as they were not able to attain full social gratification due to the lack of eye contact.

Discussions

The quantitative analysis of the pre-test and the post-test indicates a strong difference in the knowledge level of the experimental group after attending the workshop. There was a progressive growth in the entrepreneurial knowledge level of the participants after attending the two-day workshop. Apart from knowledge enhancement, the workshop also assisted the participants in gaining confidence for implementing their business ideas and to improvise their existing business set-up. The closing comments/feedback given by the participants were mostly affirmative in nature indicating the high satisfactory level of the experimental group regarding feminist social media learning system.

The central idea of feminist pedagogy is to create an empowering learning environment where the learners can construct knowledge and learn through problem-solving and self-reflection methods. In this case, learners were able to achieve this by posting their queries and collectively arriving at solutions. The content analysis of the present study clearly portrays the effectiveness of integrating feminist pedagogy to an online social media platform. It is evident from the analysis that the learners were not only able to post their questions openly, but they were also able to share and collaborate with each other, and propose many potential solutions to the problem posted.

By analysing the engagement rate of all the discussion posts and sessions of the two-day workshop, we can come to the assurance that the learners were the most interactive in the idea generation and marketing sessions. This implies that the Indian women entrepreneurs seemed to give more importance and focus on these two areas, or it can also suggest that the participants were not able to provide their inputs in other sessions due to the lack of basic knowledge or interest in them. The lack of knowledge/interest of women entrepreneurs in essential concepts such as legal registration and development of a concrete business plan might be the prime reasons behind many failures in various business ventures initiated by emerging entrepreneurs.

The network analysis shows that the participants were more interactive on the second day of the workshop when compared with the first. The increased interactivity suggests the growth in the sense of 'community' among the learners on the second day. The intensified tie-strength (the bond strength between two or more users present in a social network) between the participants (among participants and between participants and the instructor) recorded on the second day of the workshop indicates the development of a learning community within the Facebook group. Under the influence of the evolved communal learning environment, learners were able to experience secureness and confidence in voicing out their problems, experiences and opinions, heightening the knowledge sharing and collaboration process within the learning environment. The network structure also implies that on the first day of the workshop, the participants might have experienced a limited sense of security and fewer attachments to the community, resulting in the limited interaction rate.

Findings and conclusion

The study investigated the efficiency of using social media platform as a pedagogical tool to reach and educate emerging Indian women entrepreneurs. A two-day virtual workshop on entrepreneurship training was provided to the experimental group by integrating the features present in a social networking site (Facebook) and feminist pedagogy. The pretest and post-test analysis showed a constructive growth from 17% (before the workshop) to 83% in the knowledge and understanding level of basic entrepreneurial concepts among the participants after attending the workshop. The content analysis of the online discussions that occurred during the workshop showed that 38% of the comments were categorised as integration posts (collaboration and generation of potential solutions to the problems discussed), implying the effectiveness of feminist learning approach. The high satisfaction level of the participants can be derived from the extensive feedback given by them at the end of the workshop. All these key findings signify that an integrated platform built by combining social media features and feminist pedagogical techniques serves as one of the best tools for entrepreneurial training.

Overall, this research study has yielded a positive response for utilising social media platforms as an educational device. The study suggests that implementing a similar virtual learning environment at a larger level might be effective in eradicating the gender gap that is present in the educational as well as the entrepreneurial sector in India.

References

Ahl, H. 2002. "The Construction of the Female Entrepreneur as the Other." In *Casting the Other: The Production and Maintenance of Gender Inequalities in Work Organizations*, edited by B. Czarniawska and H. Höpfl, 52–67. London: Routledge.

Ahl, H. 2006. "Why Research on Women Entrepreneurs Needs New Directions." *Entrepreneurship Theory and Practice* 30 (5): 595–621.

Ajzen, I. 1991. "The Theory of Planned Behavior." *Organizational Behavior and Human Decision Processes* 50 (2): 179–211.

Alesina, A., and R. Barro. 2001. "Dollarization." *American Economic Review* 91 (2): 381–385.

Anderson, D. M., and C. J. Haddad. 2005. "Gender, Voice, and Learning in Online Course Environments." *Journal of Asynchronous Learning Networks* 9 (1): 3–14.

Anon. 2012. *The Global Entrepreneurship and Development Index, 2012. Choice Reviews Online 50, no. 01: 50-0031-50-0031.* American Library Association.

Archer, J., and B. Lloyd. 2002. *Sex and Gender*. 2nd ed. Cambridge: Cambridge University Press.

Baird, D., and M. Fisher. 2009. "Pedagogical Mash Up: Gen Y, Social Media and Learning in the Digital Age." In *Handbook of Research on New Media Literacy at the K-12 Level (Issues and Concepts)*, edited by Leo Tan Wee Hin and R. Subramaniam, 48–71. Hershey: Information Science Reference.

Balsamo, A., P. Boyer, M. Fernandes, R. Gajjala, S. Irish, A. Juhasz, E. Losh, J. Rault, and L. Wexler. 2013. *FemTechNet Whitepaper*. FemTechNet. http://femtechnet.newschool.edu/femtechnet-whitepaper/.

Baughn, C., B. L. Chua, and K. E. Neupert. 2006. "The Normative Context for Women's Participation in Entrepreneurship: A Multicountry Study." *Entrepreneurship Theory and Practice* 30 (5): 687–708.

Bertaux, N., and E. Crable. 2007. "Learning about Women. Economic Development, Entrepreneurship and the Environment in India: A Case Study." *Journal of Developmental Entrepreneurship* 12 (4): 467.

Bransford, J., A. Brown, and R. Cocking. 1999. *How People Learn*. Washington, DC: National Academy Press.

Brush, C. 2012. *Closing the Gender Gap for Women Entrepreneurs*. Forbes. http://www.forbes.com/sites/babson/2012/12/05/closing-the-gender-gap-for-women-entrepreneurs/.

Brush, C., N. Carter, E. Gatewood, P. Greene, and M. Hart. 2006. *Growth-oriented Women Entrepreneurs and Their Businesses: A Global Research Perspective*. Cheltenham: Edward Elgar Publishing.

Carney, T., M. Geertsema-Sligh, A. Savage, and A. Sluis. 2012. "Defying Borders: Transforming Learning through Collaborative Feminist Organizing and Interdisciplinary, Transnational Pedagogy." *Journal on Excellence in College Teaching* 23 (4): 127–144.

Caspi, A., E. Chajut, and K. Saporta. 2008. "Participation in Class and in Online Discussions: Gender Differences." *Computers & Education* 50 (3): 718–724.

Censusindia.gov.in. 2011. "Census of India: Primary Census Abstract". http://www.censusindia.gov.in/2011census/PCA/pca_highlights/pe_data.html.

Chick, N., and H. Hassel. 2009. "'Don't Hate Me Because I'm Virtual': Feminist Pedagogy in the Online Classroom." *Feminist Teacher* 19 (3): 195–215. http://www.jstor.org/stable/40546100.

Chinn, P. 2001. *Peace and Power*. Boston, MA: Jones and Bartlett.

Crabtree, R. 2009. *Feminist Pedagogy*. Baltimore: John Hopkins Univ. Press.

Crannie-Francies, A., W. Waring, P. Stavropoulos, and J. Kirky. 2003. *Gender Studies: Terms and Debates*. Basingstoke: Palgrave.

Delmar, F., and C. Holmquist. 2004. "Women's Entrepreneurship: Issues and Policies." Report presented at the 2nd OECD Conference of Ministers Responsible for Small and Medium-Sized Enterprises (SMEs), Turkey.

Eddleston, K. A., and G. N. Powell. 2012. "Nurturing Entrepreneurs' Work–family Balance: A Gendered Perspective." *Entrepreneurship Theory and Practice* 36 (3): 513–541.

Elliott, A. E., and V. E. Woloshyn. 1997. "Some Female Professors' Experiences of Collaboration: Mapping the Collaborative Process through Rough Terrain." *The Alberta Journal of Educational Research* 43 (1): 23–36.

Ewell, B. C. 2000. "Applying Feminist Principles to Internet-mediated Instruction: A Case Study." *Journal of Information Technology Impact*, 2 (1): 11–22.

Forsythe, D. 2003. *An Introduction to Group Dynamics*. Pacific Grove, CA: Brooks/Cole.

Garrison, D., T. Anderson, and W. Archer. 2001. "Critical Thinking, Cognitive Presence, and Computer Conferencing in Distance Education." *American Journal Of Distance Education* 15 (1): 7–23.

Glasper, A., G. McEwing, and J. Richardson. 2009. *Foundation Studies for Caring*. Palgrave: MacMillan.

Hamilton, E. 2013. "The Discourse of Entrepreneurial Masculinities (and Femininities)." *Entrepreneurship & Regional Development: An International Journal* 25: 90–99.

Hayes, E., and D. Flannery. 2000. *Women as Learners*. San Francisco, CA: Jossey-Bass.

Hezekiah, J. 1993. "Feminist Pedagogy: A Framework for Nursing Education?" *Journal of Nursing Education* 32 (2): 53–57.

Jennings, J. E., and M. S. McDougald. 2007. "Work-family Interface Experiences and Coping Strategies: Implications for Entrepreneurship Research and Practice." *Academy of Management Review* 32: 747–760.

Kaushal, D., A. Negi, and C. Singhal. 2014. "The Gender Gap in Entrepreneurship and How to Overcome It? A Study of Women Entrepreneurship Promotion in Uttarakhand State." *Global Journal of Finance and Management* 6 (2): 157–164.

Kimmel, S. 1999. "Interdisciplinary Information Searching: Moving Beyond Discipline-based Resources." In *Interdisciplinary Education: A Guide to Resources*, edited by J. Fiscella and S. Kimmel, 293–309. New York: The College Board.

Kirkup, G. 2005. "Developing Practice for Online Feminist Pedagogy." In *The Making of European Women's Studies*, edited by R. Braidotti and A. van Baren, 4, 26–40. Utrecht: Athena.Kramarae.

Kite, M. E., K. Deaux, and E. L. Haines. 2008. "Gender Stereotypes." In *Psychology of Women: A Handbook of Issues and Theories*, edited by F. L. Denma and M. A. Paludi, 2, 205–236. Westport, CT: Praeger.

Kramarae, C. 2001. *The Third Shift: Women Learning Online*. Washington, DC: American Association of University Women Educational Foundation Press.

Lai, A., and L. Lu. 2007. "Facilitative Strategies for Enhancing Knowledge Construction through Asynchronous Discussion in an Online Art Course." In *Proceedings of Society for Information Technology and Teacher Education International Conference*, edited by C. Crawford, 2673–2680. Chesapeake, VA: AACE.

Lai, A., and L. Lu. 2009. "Integrating Feminist Pedagogy with Online Teaching: Facilitating Critiques of Patriarchal Visual Culture." *Visual Culture & Gender* 4: 56–68.

Lamont, E. 2014. "Understanding the Art of Feminist Pedagogy: Facilitating Interpersonal Skills Learning For Nurses." *Nurse Education Today* 34 (5): 679–682.

Langowitz, N., and M. Minniti. 2007. "The Entrepreneurial Propensity of Women." *Entrepreneurship Theory and Practice* 31 (3): 341–364.

Lawrence, L. R. 1997. "The Interconnecting Web: Adult Learning Cohorts as Sites for Collaborative Learning, Feminist Pedagogy and Experiential Ways of Knowing." Adult Education Research Conference, Kansas.

Liñan, F., and Y. W. Chen. 2009. "Development and Cross-cultural Application of a Specific Instrument to Measure Entrepreneurial Intentions." *Entrepreneurship Theory and Practice* 33 (3): 593–617.

Liñan, F., M. A. Roomi, and F. Santos. 2010. "A Cognitive Attempt to Understanding Female Entrepreneurial Potential: The Role of Social Norms and Culture." Working paper. http://webs2002.uab.es/depeconomia-empresa/documents/10-8.pdf.

Lippa, R. A. 2005. *Gender, Nature, and Nurture*. 2nd ed. Mahwah, NJ: Erlbaum.

Maher, F. A., and M. K. Tetreault. 2008. "The Knowledge Economy and Academic Capitalism." *British Journal of Sociology of Education* 29 (6): 733–740.

Marlow, S. 2002. "Women and Self-employment: A Part of or Apart from Theoretical Construct?." *The International Journal of Entrepreneurship and Innovation* 3 (2): 83–91.

Marlow, S., and D. Patton. 2005. "All Credit To Men? Entrepreneurship, Finance and Gender." *Entrepreneurship Theory and Practice* 29: 717–735.

McMullan, F., and K. Vesgner. 2001. "Some Problems in Using Subjective Measures of Effectiveness to Evaluate Entrepreneurial Assistance Programs." *Entrepreneurship Theory and Practice* 26 (1): 37–54.

Minniti, M. 2009. "Gender Issues in Entrepreneurship." *Foundations and Trends in Entrepreneurship* 5 (7–8): 497–621.

Minniti, M., and W. Naudé. 2010. *Female Entrepreneurship across Countries and in Development*. Basingstoke: Palgrave Macmillan.

Moriano, J. A., M. Gorgievski, M. Laguna, U. Stephan, and K. Zarafshani. 2011. "A Cross-cultural Approach to Understanding Entrepreneurial Intentions." *Journal of Career Development* 38 (1): 1–24.

Nawratil, G. 1999. "Implications of Computer-Conferenced Learning for Feminist Pedagogy and Women's Studies: A Review of the Literature." *Resources for Feminist Research* 27 (1/2): 73–107.

Nelsen, R. W. 1981. "Reading, Writing, and Relationship: Toward Overcoming the Hidden Curriculum of Gender, Ethnicity, and Socio-economic Class." *Interchange* 12 (2/3): 229–242.

O' Reilly, T. 2005. *What is Web 2.0: Design Patterns and Business Models for the Next Generation of Software*. Sebastopol, CA: O' Reilly Network.

Palloff, R., and K. Pratt. 2005. "Online Learning Communities Revisited." In 21st Annual Conference on Distance Teaching and Learning, Madison, Wisconsin, USA.

Patterson, N. 2012. "Distance Education: A Perspective from Women's Studies." *International Women Online Journal Of Distance Education* 1 (2): 1–14.

Rovai, A. 2007. "Facilitating Online Discussions Effectively." *The Internet and Higher Education* 10 (1): 77–88.

Ryan, A. B. 2001. "Feminist Ways of Knowing: Towards Theorising the Person for Radical Adult Education." National Inst. of Adult Continuing Education, Leicester (England).

Sandlin, A. J. 2005. "Andragogy and its Discontents: An Analysis of Andragogy from Three Critical Perspectives." *PAACE Journal of Lifelong Learning* 14 (25): 25–42.

Sarfaraz, L., N. Faghih, and A. Asadi Majd. 2014. "The Relationship between Women Entrepreneurship and Gender Equality." *Journal of Global Entrepreneurship Research* 2 (1): 6–11.

Schniedewind, N. 1985. "Cooperatively Structured Learning: Implications for Feminist Pedagogy." *Journal of Thought* 20 (1): 74–87.

Schweitzer, I. 2001. "Women's Studies Online: Cyberfeminism or Cyberhype?" *Women's Studies Quarterly* 29 (3/4): 187–217.

Stanley-Spaeth, B. 2000. "Taming Talos: Cyberfeminist Pedagogy in Classical Studies." The World Wide Web. http://www.tulane.edu/~spaeth/talosabstract.htm.

Tambunan, T. 2009. "Women Entrepreneurship in Asian Developing Countries: Their Development and Main Constraints." *Journal of Development and Agricultural Economics* 1 (2): 27–40.

Tisdell, E. 2000. *Feminist Pedagogies. Women as Learners: The Significance of Gender in Adult Learning*. San Francisco, CA: Jossey-Bass.

Torney-Purta, J. 1983. "Psychological Perspectives on Enhancing Civic Education through the Education of Teachers." *Journal of Teacher Education* 34 (6): 30–34.

Torrens, K. M. 2007. "Disrupting Transmission: Online Learning in Gender Communication." *Transformations* 18 (1): 52–62.

Turpin, C. A. 2007. "Feminist Praxis, Online Teaching, and the Urban Campus." *Feminist Teacher* 18 (1): 9–27.

Vijay Anand, V., and N. Panchanatham. 2011. "The Thriving Women Entrepreneurs in Tamil Nadu: Motivational Factors." *Prabandhan: Indian Journal Of Management* 4 (8): 44.

Waris, A., and B. Viraktamath. 2013. "Gender Gaps and Women's Empowerment in India – Issues and Strategies." *International Journal of Scientific and Research Publications* 3 (9): 1–9.

Webb, L. M., M. W. Allen, and K. L. Walker. 2002. "Feminist Pedagogy: Identifying Principles." *Academic Education Quarterly* 6: 67–72.

Wilson, F., J. Kickul, and D. Marlino. 2007. "Gender, Entrepreneurial Self-Efficacy, and Entrepreneurial Career Intentions: Implications for Entrepreneurship Education." *Entrepreneurship Theory and Practice* 31 (3): 387–406.

Winn, J. 2005. "Women Entrepreneurs: Can We Remove the Barriers?" *The International Entrepreneurship and Management Journal* 1 (3): 381–397.

Index

age 39, 56, 57, 59, 64, 66, 69, 72, 75, 89
Ajzen, I. 82
Akins, F. 50
Alesina, A. 80
Allen, M. W. 89
Anderson, T. 91
Archer, W. 91
Autumn, R. R. 50

Ball, S. 62
Barro, R. 80
blended 1, 7, 31, 47, 51, 56
Brush, C. 81
Burge, E. 50
Burke, P. J. 61

capitalist economies 5
Carney, T. 84
Check, E. 50
Chick, N. 36, 86
classroom/ conventional classroom/ classroom - physical space 1–4, 7, 11, 14–16, 19–20, 22–23, 25–26, 30, 32, 34, 63, 66, 69, 72–73, 84–86
Clegg, S. 56
collaborative learning 86
communication 11, 12
consumerism 43, 44
content analysis 91–92
correspondence education 10; *see also* distance education
critical consciousness 11
critical pedagogies 91
cyber-ethnography 36
cyberfeminist pedagogy 36
cyber space/internet 25, 35, 36, 47, 48, 50, 58, 59

Daniels, J. 36
Davies, J. 36
democratization 1, 2, 4, 5, 31, 37, 42, 44, 51
digital revolution 8
disenfranchised learners 1
distance education 1–19, 22, 55, 73, 75, 76; positive distance of 24–26

education 4, 12, 13; *see also* distance education; higher education; online education
entrepreneurs 1
entrepreneurship 80
expert educator 60

Facebook 97
face-to-face teaching 1
false dichotomy 36
feminist classroom 84
feminist distance education: models of 17–18
feminist education literature 11
feminist ethics 4
feminist pedagogical initiatives: at Open University (OU) 18–22
feminist pedagogies 1, 3, 5–7, 10–26, 37–39, 75–77, 80–103; Web 2.0, integration 86–87
first-generation distance learning programmes 12

Flannery, D. 88
for-profit schools 55
Freire, P. 34, 76
Freixas, A. 59, 76

Gajjala, R. 36
Garrison, D. 91
gender 1–4, 6, 7, 9, 21, 82; and entrepreneurship 82–83
Gender and Education 2
gender dynamics 5
gender gap 4–6, 8, 80, 81, 103
gender power 12
gender relations 12
gender-sensitive technology-enhanced learning 10–26
gender stereotypes 18
geographical space 33
gerontology 55–77
Global Entrepreneurship Monitor 81

Hassel, H. 36, 86
Hayes, E. 88
Haywood, C. 58
Henderson, E. F. 15
Herman, C. 6
higher education (HE) 1, 4, 5, 7, 8, 30, 32, 37, 39, 42, 55–77, 83, 87
hijra community 47
Hofstede, G. 11
hooks, b. 2, 35, 63
Huang Hoon, C. 35
humour 63
hybrid 7, 32, 36, 51, 56

ideologies 55–77
IGNOU/ Indira Gandhi National Open University 7, 39–40, 47–48, 51–52
India 4, 5, 7, 31, 32, 37–40, 44, 46, 47, 49, 51, 80, 81, 83, 87–89, 94, 98, 103
Indian women 80, 81, 83, 87, 89, 98, 101, 102
inéditos viáveis 57–60
inédito viável 63–72
international 1, 2, 6, 7, 31, 37, 46, 51, 61, 66

Jackson, S. 17

Kaushal, D. 81
Kendall, L. 35, 59
Kimmel, S. 84
Kirkup, G. 6, 21–22, 34, 38, 86
Koenig-Visagie, L. 38
Kramarae, C. 87

Larreamendy-Joerns, J. 37, 39
Leander, K. M. 36
learners 1–3, 7, 11, 13, 14, 17, 18, 23, 30, 31, 33–35, 41, 42, 47–49, 83–88, 91, 92, 101, 102
Leinhardt, G. 37, 39
Lenskyi, H. 50
liberation theories 14
Luque, B. 59, 76

Mac an Ghaill, M. 58
Maher, F. A. 84
Maher, J. 35
MA in Women's & Gender Studies (MAWGS) programme 40, 44
Malcolm, I. 17
marginalized learners 1
masculinities 1, 3, 7, 8, 46, 47, 55–77
McKim, K. K. 36
McMullan, F. 90
minimum viable product (MVP) 92, 93
mixed-sex tutor groups 19
Mohanty, C. T. 5, 34
Moore, M. G. 12, 16, 33
Morley, L. 14
Murray Jessica, D. B. 38

nationalist patriarchy 50
Negi, A. 81
newest feminist pedagogy 24–26
New Women's Movement 81
Noble, D. 5
non-profit schools 55

online 1, 3–6, 8, 19, 20, 56
online education 55–77
Online Workshop for Professional Entrepreneurial Training for Women (OWPETW) 89, 97, 99
open and distance 1, 4, 5
Open & Distance Learning (ODL) pedagogies 31–39

Open Educational Resource (OER) 22
Open University, U.K. 7, 10, 33, 38–39, 52

Patterson, N. 3, 34, 37
pedagogy 14
personal/experiential knowledge 14
placed resources 5
positive action 16–17
post-colonial feminism 50
potential misunderstanding 12
Prinsloo, M. 5, 36
programme-based illustration 40–42
psychological space 6, 12, 20, 33, 56

quantitative analysis 92–97

reconciling feminist pedagogy 30–51
Reina, A. 59, 76
reminiscence 71
Richards, R. S. 36
Rovai, A. 85
Rowbotham, I. 21–22
Rybas, N. 36

Schweitzer, I. 36, 83
science and technology 16, 23
science, technology, engineering, and maths (STEM) subjects 16, 18, 20, 23
self-learning materials (SLMs) 35
Sex Discrimination Act 1975 17
Simpson, O. 13
Singhal, C. 81
social media 8, 80–103
social network analysis (SNA) 91, 97–100
social web 85–86
substantive transformations 37

teachers/educators 2, 3, 6–12, 14–16, 22–24, 30, 31–35, 38, 56, 57, 60, 63, 69, 72, 73, 75, 89
teaching-learning environments 3
technology-enhanced learning 6, 10, 24, 26
Tetreault, M. K. 84
Thomas, K. 17
traditional HE spaces 55–57
transactional distance 3, 6–7, 10–26, 36
transgressive education 35

vanguard space 8
Vesgner, K. 90
virtual 1–5, 7, 8, 15, 30, 31, 36, 87
virtual pedagogies 2, 5
Von Prummer, C. 34

Walker, K. L. 89
Ward, K. J. 36
Webb, L. M. 89
Web 2.0 tools 85–86; and feminist pedagogy 86–87
Whitelegg, E. 21, 38
Whitelegg, L. 21–22
women 1, 10–11, 16–19, 21, 34, 36; entrepreneurs 80–103; gender/power on 12; students, impact 22–24; studies, managing at ODL 39–50
Women in Technology (WIT) scheme 18, 19
Women into Management 20
Women's & Gender Studies (WGSs) 21, 38
workshop, feedback 100–101

For Product Safety Concerns and Information please contact our EU representative GPSR@taylorandfrancis.com Taylor & Francis Verlag GmbH, Kaufingerstraße 24, 80331 München, Germany